Job Security for Life in Teaching

Teaching

How to become an online tutor

Joanne Kaminski

ISBN-10: 0988930110
ISBN-13: 978-0-9889301-1-7

DEDICATION

This book is dedicated to all of the amazing teachers out there that continue to do what they love on a daily basis whether it is online or in the classroom. You are my hero.

Table of Contents

ACKNOWLEDGMENTS

I would like to Acknowledge Mike Koenigs, Paul Colligan, Ed Rush, and Pam Hendrickson for believing in my idea and pushing me to make this a reality.

I would like to thank my husband and kids for all of their support with my career choices and the love that they give me on a daily basis.

A huge thanks goes out to my business partner Renee Love for all of the help that she provides with formatting, book covers, and logos. I admire her talent

.

Do You Need Help Becoming an Online Tutor?

This book contains some of the most influential tools that I have utilized to start my own tutoring company. Because I was once where you are today, I want to give you a whole bunch of free stuff to grow your business. We are all out there to support each other and help out in any way possible. My mission is to help new online tutors and online tutors that have been struggling with starting their own online tutoring business to become as successful as they believe possible.

To help you out I have created a whole goodie bag of free stuff for you.

- Videos with tools you can begin using today.
- Special invites to webinars.
- Special invites to conferences.
- And a whole bunch of other cool stuff.

Does that sound awesome or what? Get instant access at

www.tutorpreneurs.com/free-videos

Introduction

Congratulations! You have most likely picked up this book because being an online tutor or teacher is a career choice that intrigues you. We are very similar because it intrigued me as well.

At one point in time people became teachers because it was a not only their passion to teach, but because it was a safe market. The facts are simple, schools are in every town across the world. On top of that the benefits are really good. However, times are changing. That idea of job security in teaching is changing as well.

In fact the changes in the economy are resulting in a smaller amount of money that can be given to the schools. This in turn is leading to budget cuts. With budget cuts, comes staff cuts. With staff cuts comes this feeling of insecurity. People are now wondering if their job is safe and if they will be the next one to be cut.

Class sizes seem to be getting bigger and more and more responsibilities are placed on teachers than have ever been placed before. Teachers are becoming burnt out quicker and being forced to leave a profession they once saw themselves doing for the rest of their lives.

There is hope though. See, teachers will always be needed. Kids will always need to learn and they need people who know how to teach. The educational system is changing and with that change comes a natural fear. People don't know what classrooms will look like. Will it all be virtual based or partially virtually based? Who knows. The point is with change there is always fear. People begin to think of what their role will be in the future of education and where they would like their role to be.

Have you ever dreamed of being able to wake up in the morning, pour your coffee, and go to your office in your house and start teaching for the day. Sounds like a dream, right? No early wake up calls, no commute, and no hassle. Just the ease and comfort of working from your own home. Ahhh!

Well, this can be a reality for people who dream about this. More and more teachers are dreaming about this reality because it leaves politics out the door and gets back to basics of being able to just teach kids.

What if you could teach kids in a one on one fashion, giving them what they need, when they need it. What if it could be that easy as to pour that coffee, come to your at home office, and start helping kids in the area that you love teaching most? Would you want to know more about that?

My name is Joanne Kaminski and I had this same dream. I had no idea how to turn this dream into a reality and then one day all of the answers seemed to come to me as to how it really could work. I was so excited about turning this dream into a reality, but there was fear involved. That fear I had to put on the backburner while I made a go at it.

Many people each year try to make a go at this dream and don't get very far. They let some of the stumbling blocks become boulders and quit. They let fear stop them from accomplishing their dream. Voices inside their head tell them that this can't be done. People tell them that kids need in person teaching because online teaching is impersonal and therefore ineffective. Those voices inside your head and those people are all wrong.

I have created systems to turn this dream into a reality not only for myself, but for you as well. I have had to learn the hard way, by digging my feet in, working hard, and doing a whole bunch of things wrong before I knew how to do them right.

Today I have a huge gift for you. You don't need to learn the hard way like I did. Follow me and I will guide you in how to do it the easy way. I will share with you the 4 step system that I have used to make this an easy lifestyle. A lifestyle that allows me to bring my job with me anywhere in the world. A lifestyle that allows me to be a mom that is around to raise my own children. A lifestyle that is something way beyond anything that I could ever have dreamed of.

I am not going to keep this 4 step system a secret. I am going to begin by sharing it with you right from the start. Then I am going to share my story with you and why I am qualified to teach you these systems. Then I am going to give you tools that you can begin using right away if you really want to become an online tutor in any field.

The 4 step system to being a profitable online tutor includes;

1. MINDSET

2. Organized Systems

3. Powerful Marketing

4. SERVICES

A different MINDSET is needed if you are considering online tutoring or teaching as a career choice. This wasn't a career choice that even existed when we were kids. Certainly a different MINDSET is needed when it comes to how much money we can make. A different MINDSET is needed from having a job, to a career, to a business. A different MINDSET is needed to create your own success.

In order to be successful you need to have systems in place. A business that is not well thought out and not organized will fail. Businesses that are not organized put their chances in luck instead of what has been proven to work. They don't take the steps that they need to take to be successful. Being an online tutor requires these effective systems.

Online tutors need to have a powerful Marketing strategy. Many of the online tutors out there today just put themselves on lists that never get them found. This book will give you tools right out of the gate to get found by the people you want to find you. People who get started in this career think that if they make a website, that people will find them accidentally on the web. This is just not true. You will learn powerful Marketing strategies that will get you found and have more students than you are able to SERVICE on your own.

Lastly, you need to be able to provide online SERVICES that deliver the end result to the client. If a child is struggling in reading, and you are a reading tutor, then you need to increase their reading level. You will learn how to provide SERVICES that people want you to provide for their child. You will stand out amongst the crowd and become competition and recession proof.

This industry according to businesswire.com is projected to be a $100 billion a year industry[1] by the year 2017. As you know children are being faced with higher standards everyday. This means that there is more of a need of online tutoring and teaching than has ever been needed before. The pot is big enough for you to find the clientele that you want to SERVICE and to provide those SERVICES better than others out there.

Not only are you going to learn about these systems in this book, but you are also going to get answers to the most frequently asked questions and the most frequent fears that people have. Some of those questions are, "How successful can an online tutoring business be?" Another one is, "Where will I get students from?" The big one is about the bottom line. "How much will it cost me to start my own business as an online tutor and run it?"

All of those answers and more will be given in this book. Now the only question left is, are you ready to dive in with me and take the journey of your life?

---

[1] http://www.businesswire.com/news/home/20110722005211/en/Private-Tutoring-Market-Witness-Huge-Growth-Reach

Step I

MINDSET

1 An Inside peek at my foundation and early belief systems

I was born and raised in a small town called Auburn, Massachusetts. Growing up my dad was a machinist at a local manufacturing firm called ATF Davidson. He was making what he would consider good money, but the workers there were unionized and would go on strike all of the time. My mom stayed home and took care of me for a few years, but soon she found herself having to get a part time job working at a restaurant close to home called Friendly's. Both of my parents worked hard and taught me all about a good work ethic. Their philosophy was, "Anything worth doing is worth doing well."

One thing that I did not realize growing up was that this world consists of people with two different MINDSETs. There are the people who work their butts off for a little amount of money and there are people who seem to attract money easily and efficiently. I grew up in a family that worked their butt off.

My mom instilled this value that whatever I do, I should do it well. When it came to grades I didn't always get the best ones, but my mom would always ask me if I tried my best. When I told her that

I did, she would say, "That is the only thing that I can ask of you." The good thing is that I knew that I was always going to make my mom happy no matter what I did or what I accomplished. I never felt like I had to prove my worth to her, because in her eyes I was perfect the way I was.

We had very little money growing up. I would always see my dad stressed out about it or my mom stressed out about it. Many fights in our household revolved around money and I can only imagine the fear that arose because of the lack of money. There was fear on being able to pay the bills and there was so much fear that my mom fell into a state of manic depression. When she was manic she would spend crazily and when she was depressed she would sleep all the time.

One day the company that my dad worked for closed down. He went from making decent money to making much less money.

As a direct result, my mom got a full time job at a car insurance company. She hated her job and complained every single day that she came home from work. She clearly was not happy with the deck of cards that life seemed to have dealt her.

Every day when she went to work she had the wonderful opportunity to talk to people who were in a car accident. They wanted to be able to get money and when my mom would have to say no, they would yell at her. So all day long she listened to people yell at her. Or, at least that was my understanding as a child.

I didn't want to take that path. I didn't want to work in a job that I hated. I didn't want to work at a job that didn't paid very well. In fact, I knew from an early age that I was going to be rich. I would tell my dad when he told me to pick something up that I would do it later. He would tell me that he was training me for later on in life and I always responded that I was just going to hire a maid, so I didn't need that training. He would laugh at me and tell me good luck and say that will never happen. (Don't worry, I did grow out of that lazy syndrome and I am very proud of the successes I have achieved.)

The only way that I could conceive of making money was by getting a job since that was what I had been programmed to believe. My grandparents had jobs, my parents had jobs, and all of my friends parents had typical jobs. So, I always saw myself as getting a job. But not just any job, I was going to be a LAWYER. I thought that was where all of the money was. I had a friend one time tell me that she was going to be a lawyer, so I had figured that if she could be a lawyer, then so could I. I really didn't have any other reasoning for why I wanted to be a lawyer other than you could make a lot of money and I wanted to be better than she was.

My dad supported this idea and thought that I would make a really great lawyer. Every time we got into an argument he would tell me that my arguing skills would come in very handy as a lawyer. I actually took this as a compliment and as fuel for keeping this dream alive to become a lawyer.

I began looking at schools to attend for college and other schools that had a good law program. I chose Marquette University because I had heard they had a good pre-law program and a law school.

I was so excited about going to college and starting this chapter of my life. My first year in college I decided to join a group called the Mock Trial group. I had never been part of something like this before, but I enjoyed it thoroughly with all of the acting that was involved.

However, there was one small problem that I found out about law that didn't fit my moral standards. When I learned that lawyers need to protect their clients even if they know their client is guilty I realized that this was not the career path for me.

I could not get over that sinking feeling I had deep in my heart that actually made me sick when I thought of it. When I thought about major crimes that people could have committed that they could get off of because of my skills as a lawyer, I realized that I did not want to continue on this path anymore. My morals where something that I treasured and you couldn't pay me enough money to put them on the back burner.

I had to reinvent what my career path was going to look like. I really struggled with this process because ever since 6th grade I had pretty much made up my mind about what I was going to do.

I remember one day walking on the Marquette campus between the Union and the dorm I lived in. I thought, "Hmmm, what is something that I am good at?" Then it came to me. I remember my mom saying that I was really good with kids. So, I began to think about career paths that involved kids.

My desire to become a teacher was born that day. I remember when I told my parents that the expensive education that they had worked their butt off to help me pay for was really going to result in large dividends for them because I was going to become a teacher.

That was not a pleasant conversation. For the first time in my life, my parents were not happy about the decisions that I was making. I think that they had bought into this idea that I could become a lawyer. To go from a career path that could result in really good money to working as a teacher was not their proudest moment for me.

My aunt had been a teacher and my mom and dad had not communicated with her in a while because of land disputes, so whether their dislike of this career path was because of their perception of her or because of money is unknown till this day.

As a student in education I really had found my happy spot. I really enjoyed the classes and what I had decided to do with my life. I moved off campus my 3rd year with my future husband. In order to pay for the apartment I got a part time job working for Warner Brothers Studio Store. I loved this job and did the best that I could do from day 1.

I was soon promoted to a key holder and from there an assistant manager. I was now working full time and going to school full time. I had very little time to sleep, but I loved both positions. I was literally a student by day and a sales associate by night.

I had seen myself as staying in this position after college because I loved it so much. The atmosphere was fun and I was really good at it. However, the store was not making the kinds of sales that warranted keeping it open. So, the company closed this particular location down.

I had graduated from college by this time and had missed my opportunity to do my student teaching. So, I decided to get another job as an assistant manager at another retail store.

American Eagle Outfitters hired me and I felt like I was on my way up in the world as another Assistant Manager. However, this work environment was not as much fun as Warner Brothers had been and I worked with a bunch of high school students that didn't seem to have the same work ethic that I had. It was frustrating and it felt like babysitting instead of running a business.

So, I decided to go back to finish up my student teaching the following year. I worked in an inner city school that consisted of 50% students with disabilities. Most of the disabilities in the classroom were children that had autism and I had the opportunity to learn so much about how to adapt instruction to meet the needs of all of the students.

While I was doing my student teaching I needed to get a job because I had to pay money to be a student teacher. So I got another job as a waitress at a restaurant. I would work all day at the school teaching and then after that go straight to Champ's Americana to make some money as a waitress. Even my husband worked there on the weekend to earn some extra money to pay the bills.

This entire six months that I had done my student teaching had been grueling. I was working from 7:00am to 5:00pm at school and then I would go to work from 5:30pm till 11:30pm and wake up in the morning to do it all over again. I wasn't the best student teacher in the world because I was constantly tired. Always being on the go like that will do that to you. Along with having someone study your every move, a.k.a. the classroom teacher, was not always easy either.

I finished up my student teaching, continued working as a waitress and got a full time job as a substitute teacher in the suburbs. I was an o.k. substitute teacher, not the best, but one of the teachers saw a lot of potential in me. She told me that there was a position in the school opening up as a Kindergarten teacher and that I should apply. She thought that I would have a good chance at the job since I was already substituting. I did not get the job. Instead a relative of the principal got the job. Yes, knowing the right people gets you jobs, even in teaching. We all thought that this was unfair, but one of the things that my mom taught me was, "Sometimes, life is not fair."

2 Teaching in the School System

"Sometimes life is not fair." That pretty much sums up my first year of teaching that no one could have every prepared me for. Although, I must preference that everything that I went through was exactly the way it was supposed to be. I needed to experience everything that I experienced in order to be where I am at today.

So I applied for teaching positions and was starting to get nervous because by July of 2000 I didn't have a teaching job. So I began working as a camp counselor for the YMCA. During the summer I applied to some more teaching jobs and ended up at a job interview at a school in the inner city of Milwaukee. The school was a start up charter school. I had no idea what my life was going to be like working at a start up school and I had no idea what my life was going to be like working at a Charter school. I nailed my interview and was offered $30,000 to start teaching my first year and was told that it would be in a 3rd grade classroom.

The principal for the school was apparently super successful at other start up schools in California. So there seemed to be some hope with that thought. (Later on you will learn that she didn't last past October.)

I received a letter from the school that had my signed contract in it and in that letter I was informed that I would need to bring my own lawn chair because the chairs had not been unpacked yet. I laughed at this thought because it hadn't dawned on me that nothing had actually been set up yet and the school was starting in 1 month.

So I went to that meeting with my lawn chair and that feeling of not being comfortable being in a new setting consumed me. I sat down next to someone that I had met at a staff event a week earlier in the summer. Honestly I don't remember much about what they talked about that day. The only things that I actually remember are that they wanted all of us to unpack all of the curriculum, stamp it, and put the furniture together so that we could be up and going on day one. I wasn't really expecting that, but since I am a team player I helped out as much as I could.

That day they gave us our room assignments and I was excited to see what my first classroom was going to look like. I took pictures of my first classroom and it was completely empty. The first thing that stuck out was that there were no windows. I had never been in a classroom that had no windows so this was new for me. My colleagues and I joked about painting a window up on our wall to make the situation better, but none of us actually did that.

The building for our school had previously been a hospital. So on my wall was a steel cabinet that had no shelves. Apparently, I was in the old maternity ward and that awkward cabinet was used as some kind of refrigeration.

I remember brainstorming and beginning to think of ways to turn that into a closet since there was no other place in the classroom to store things. Once the math supplies were delivered I neatly organized them in this storage cabinet that my husband so kindly helped me create.

So now I had math supplies all neatly organized in this cabinet, but I didn't have any furniture. That meant, no desks for the kids, no desks for the teachers, no chairs, and nothing else that I needed in order to get things up and running in my classroom.

The only thing that I could do at that point was go to the space that was called the old auditorium and help unpack all of the boxes, stamp all of the materials, and help put the furniture together. This was a great opportunity to meet other teachers and get to know them.

I learned about the level of experiences that all of the other teachers had and realized that beyond the lead teachers, most of us were first year teachers. We didn't have a clue of how to teach, how to manage a classroom, and how to deal with complex situations when they arose.

The lead teachers had a ton of experience teaching, so they were pretty much our go to person to contact when we needed support. The lead teacher for my team had grown up on an airport base with her dad and had 30 years of teaching experience. Everything was very cut and dry for her. She was concerned about details being in place on day one that I never would have thought about like making sure all of the kids had the same heading on each of their papers. I honestly didn't see this as an important topic, but sat and listened anyway. My thought was as long as the kids had their name on the paper and their teachers name, then all was good. Heck if the kid could remember to put his/her name on the paper, then life would be good, right? It seemed like there were bigger things that we needed to tackle, such as, what would day one look like and what did we need to do to make it all go smoothly.

I didn't add a lot of feedback in the meetings because honestly the topics seemed mundane to what I needed to accomplish. I had no thoughts to add to the topics, so I sat and listened. This was not looked on well from my lead teacher and one day as I was leaving the building she tracked me down in the parking lot. She was not happy with me and in fact she scared me with her military cold demeanor. She said that I wasn't a team player and that I needed to add feedback to the group.

I remember feeling angry about this because the topics being discussed were not things that I needed to be a part of. My room still needed to get ready and I still didn't have desks. There was only 1 week left and I was getting the teaching walls organized for the content that would be going up there.

I was now a frustrated team member. I continued to put everyone else's furniture together without having any furniture in my classroom. I continued to attend these meetings that dealt with topics such as, where the kids should write their name on the paper. Should it be on the right hand side or the left hand side?

Anxiety and excitement were part of the core of my being. 5 days left. Still no furniture. Then the big moment arrived. One desk began to arrive after another. No chairs, but it was a start. The first day of school was becoming more of a reality for me.

Eventually I had a teacher's desk, chair, and about 20 student desks. Ahhhh, I was beginning to feel much better. Everything might actually be in place for day 1 of school.

I knew that in order for me to run my classroom effectively I needed to start putting all of my time and energy on creating SYSTEMS and expectations that were going to work in my classroom. I knew the importance of starting out right the first couple of days of school so that I could teach my kids for the rest of the year.

I began thinking about how I was going to greet my students as they first entered and what the first activity was going to be. I had created a personalized word search with all of the students names. This way when the student got into the classrooms we could introduce ourselves and they would immediately become engaged in the activity. This gave me the opportunity to make the best first impression with each one of them as they slowly entered the classroom.

I felt confident about day 1. After a couple of school-wide meetings about procedures for the first day of school, I felt confident that I knew what to do, what to expect, and what I was going to teach. However, nothing could have prepared me for what was about to be in store.

I had 20 chairs and 25 kids listed on my roster. It was day one of school and I was becoming a little bit anxious that these kids were not going to have a place to call their home, a.k.a. their desk, when they arrived. I imagined how weird that would be for the student and really wanted to have enough desks for everyone.

I called the office and a savior had come to my rescue. She couldn't give me desks, but she said that she knew where there were some chairs. So she had 5 more chairs delivered to my classroom. I had a couple of tables so the kids could just sit at the tables until the desks were ready.

The classroom was going to be very tight and I was told that there would not be any more students added to our classroom. So even though it was tight, I knew that we could make it work. I love focusing on solutions instead of problems, so I knew we could make it work.

Day one arrived and the students began to trickle into the classroom. I turned my back to write something on the board and I was met by this sharp pain in my back. I had no idea what it was so I turned around and there was a young man poking me to get my attention with a sharp pencil. I was taken aback by this greeting and turned around to get him to stop. He had a question and I answered it, but I was left with this impression of what the heck.

About every half hour I was interrupted by the office that day for the first 4 hours that they were adding more students to my class. I was starting to get nervous again because I didn't have any desks or chairs for the student. When I told the office this, it didn't seem to matter, and they would send the student anyway. So, there where students that needed to sit on the floor or stand. This was not a pretty situation. The kids were getting irritated with each other and they were kicking each other and yelling at each other. No fights broke out in my room that day, but they did while the students were in specials.

As the office continued to send more and more students more mayhem was breaking out. I remember my anxiety being so high that I told the office they were not allowed to send another student unless there was a desk and a chair for them. My opinion had no weight and they continued to send students anyway. At the end of the day there were 32 students in my classroom, very angry children and very little was accomplished.

The kids went home and all I remember doing was crying. How in the world had I ever gotten myself into a career where this could be my reality. There had to be a better way.

I wasn't the only one who felt this way. I had really connected with some other first year teachers and that night we all went out to the bar for some drinks. We talked about our first day and each of our situations and I wasn't the only one who had a day from hell. My story was no different, but I left feeling like tomorrow had to be better. This was complete insanity in my mind.

I called the teacher of the classroom that I had done my student teaching with and shared with her my first day experience and asked for her advice. She pretty much told me to start the next day as if nothing had happened the first day and start all over again. I thought that was great advice and decided to put that into action.

The next day came and I started it all over as if nothing had happened the day before. As the kids entered the classroom I took each of their pictures with the nameplates they had designed the day before. I thought this would help me learn all 32 names quickly. Nothing is more difficult than having students without a desk in your classroom AND you can't even refer to them by name. My purpose was to memorize their face and their name so that the next day I would know everyone.

That day did not go as expected or planned either. It was complete mayhem again and the kids were making so much noise that they couldn't even hear me. There were times that I had to resort to a blowing a whistle. I felt that this was the only way to get their attention because they were so loud.

After a few days of using my whistle I was banned from using it from the administration and I was a complete wreck. I had no idea how I was going to be able to teach the classroom. So far the only thing that we had tackled was classroom management, classroom management, and more classroom management. We practiced what it would look like to get in line with our hands behind our back so that we couldn't cause problems with them. We practiced walking in the hallway without talking and they would continue to talk and talk and talk. I tried positive reinforcement, negative reinforcement , and everything in between to find something that would work.

Then one day I tried using my voice and I was yelling at the students. I couldn't believe that I had resorted to this, but it was the only thing that got their attention and worked.

My classroom was home to the following students.

1. A gifted and talented kid that when he didn't get the right kind of attention would go over to the steel cabinet and bang his head to the point where there was blood.

2. A child that not only threatened to kill his mom, but brought a bike chain to school and threatened to choke all of the other kids in the hallway when I wasn't looking.

3. The largest 3rd grader I had ever seen that fought every single day.

4. A girl that talked back to me every time I had a conversation with her and would laugh at me and get the other kids to laugh at me.

5. I had one white girl who was sweet, shy, and developed so much anxiety she developed an ulcer from the classroom conditions.

6. One child that who would join in any fight that occurred and get in the middle of it.

7. A set of twins that teamed up against the music teacher and threatened physical assault because the teacher put her hand on her to direct her to the back of the line. The cops were brought in and the teacher was put on a plan.

8. Another little boy that was sweeter than pie, super smart, but had an extreme temper that would explode on the other kids at any moment. He was involved in just as many fights as the rest of them.

9. The kid that would pee if he didn't get his way

10. A homeless student that refused to sit in a chair and would only sit under his desk and crawl on the floor like a baby for the entirety of the day.

11. The smartest girl in the class showed up 1 or 2 times a week. The other 3-4 days a week her mom had her stay home so that she could take care of the baby.

12. The runner who would just walk up and leave and never come back.

Now you may be thinking that this sounds like complete insanity and believe me it was. The good news for me was that I was not alone. Everyone was experiencing behaviors like these, so while I thought my classroom was different it really wasn't.

Substitute teachers would come in and they would share their stories of how they had to put their bodies up against the door so that the kids wouldn't just run out of the classroom. I had runners, but I had no idea of how to solve that. If I had a child run out of the classroom, then I would call the office and let them know.

One time I had a kid run out of my classroom, run into other classrooms and steal the kids supplies right of their desk and then run into another classroom and do the same thing. One time security found him running in the halls and he threw all the stolen supplies down the stairs and continued running.

I literally felt like I was in a mental institute for children. I was making home visits and trying to come up with solutions with the parents for the types of behavior that we were dealing with. I was not met with a warm smile. I could hear comments as I would be approaching the door like, "What's that white teacher doing here?" I would be met by a woman with a baby in her hands and the kids completely out of control in the background. The music would by blaring and the TELEVISION's were all on. It was not an environment that I was used to and I was clearly not welcomed into these neighborhoods.

Every minute that I had a free moment I was trying to problem solve and brainstorm solutions to the problems we were having in the classroom while the other kids were in specials. I had no planning time because I was trying to solve all of these problems, with very little success. I was not allowed to send kids out of the classroom unless there was a fight or something major was going on, so the smaller problems had to all be dealt with by me.

Now let's top all of that with one of the biggest problems. Only 20% of the students in my classroom could actually read at grade level. Wow, so I have all of this content that I needed to teach these kids and they were not capable of actually understanding when they read it. Everything had to be modified. Not only is this all new content for me to learn how to teach, but now it had to be modified so that the kids could learn it. I was easily putting in 12 hours a day and working on the weekends to correct all of the papers.

I did not have a healthy MINDSET. The first two weeks were spent with me crying and having no real solutions that worked. After the first two weeks of crying the crying became less frequent, but it still continued throughout the year.

I eventually learned how to manage the classroom through a raffle system. I had a bingo ball with numbers and every student had a number. I would call a number and if the student was doing what they were supposed to be doing at that moment they would get to pick from the prize box. Phew finally I had a system in place that while it was only temporary it was something. And that was my first year of teaching. A roller-coaster of an experience physically and mentally.

I didn't think that I was going to come back to this school the following year. During the first half of the year we had already had 50% teacher turnover rate. Teachers were quitting left and right and substitutes were put into place until they could hire someone. Some of those teachers only lasted 1 day to 2 weeks. It was crazy. Even the principals position was a revolving door. Our first year had resulted in 3 different administrators.

At the end of the school year my own life had been hit my tragedy. My dad had died completely unexpectedly at the age of 52. So I was too distraught to find another job. Surprisingly on top of that, this school actually wanted me to come back because I had made it the whole year without quitting.

This situation ended up being the biggest blessing I had every received. I started off the next school year and my classroom management skills were top notch. I took a course called Anger

Management to learn how to deal with all of the anger that these students were seeming to have, but I really learned how to keep my own anger in check and be a better teacher.

At the end of that year, I was so good at teaching reading that I was asked to train other teachers how to teach the reading program all over the country. I was so good at that that I was asked the following year to teach the trainers and the teachers along with have my own classroom. It was a lot AND I was loving every second of it. I LOVED teaching. I LOVED that I could manage my classroom and teach these kids. It was rewarding, but that third year I became pregnant and my world was about to change once again. As much as I loved teaching, I wanted to be a mom to my little girl. I was still teaching, training all over the country, but this beautiful baby girl was not getting the time that she deserved with her mommy. So the following year I was offered the Reading Curriculum Coordinator's position. I could work 35 hours, go home and not have any homework to correct and be a mom to my little girl. It seemed like a win-win to me, so I stuck around for a few more years.

I continued this position for 5 years and had two more babies. That desire to be a mom and be there more and more for my own girls was just killing me inside. I had a long drive to and from work, worked 35 hours. With the drive it was still well over 40 hours a week. When you are missing your kids, that is long time to be away from them.

I had this strong desire for balance and I did not have it, nor did I know how to get it. So after working at this school for 8 years I decided to work closer to home. I had already gone to school now to get my master's and was a certified reading teacher and a Reading Specialist. So I got a job as a Reading Specialist at a school in Waukesha that was only 15 minutes from home. I still didn't have that balance and I was completely unhappy teaching other teachers how to teach reading instead of working with students myself.

25

I got sick that year and it took me out of the school system for 3 months. I was in and out of the hospital for 6 months and a diagnosis was never discovered. When I finally arrived back to work, I got written up for having energy levels that were all over the place. This was the straw that broke the camels back. I realized that I was putting my heart and sole into something that wasn't giving me anything back in return. It was time for me to decide what I really wanted in my life.

I had just read the Secret and had the empowering MINDSET that I could be, do and have whatever I wanted. What I wanted more than anything else was to be an online reading teacher, so that I could be there for my own little girls and continue to do what I loved to do most. Teach kids how to read easily and effortlessly.

Now I have come up with SYSTEMS that have turned this dream into a reality. I am able to be home for my kids when they are sick. I am able to be there before and after school and I am able to be active in their education as a room mom. When I am not with them, I am teaching kids how to read online in a back to back format so that I can be there for my own kids when they need me. I no longer have to deal with all of that classroom management stuff in order to teach. I can teach kids to read and get results quickly. In fact my students are able to close the gap a full year with 8-12 hours of instruction. This kind of teaching method has never existed before and I want to teach as many teachers as I can this easy simple method so that kids all over the world can benefit.

So, that was teaching in the school system for me. I had found that it wasn't really where my heart was. I had this tugging in my heart that I was meant to do something else, but even though I wanted to teach online, I didn't know that was what it actually was. I had to try doing a whole bunch of stuff that I didn't like in order to find what I truly love. You will learn about these failed business ventures in the next chapter.

3 Five failed Businesses

"Success is going from failure to failure without losing enthusiasm."
– Winston Churchill

I would love to say that the first time I tried to run a business that I knew exactly what I was doing and was successful right out of the gate. But, that was not the case and I consider myself a pretty smart person. This is the whole reason I want to share SYSTEMS with you that will help you start your business easily and efficiently. If you have picked up this book, then you also are a pretty smart person and I don't want you to have to go through the learning curve that I did. I would like to help speed up the process for you and make it as easy as possible.

The first business that I failed at was trying to make money on ebay. I specifically sold used clothing that was in great condition. I sold the clothing in lots thinking this would make it more valuable. With all of the shipping costs this endeavor landed me in the hole. I had tried to read all of the books out there that would help me launch this successfully, but honestly I think the whole ebay craze, where it might have been profitable for small business owners like me at one time, was beginning to lose it's steam. I tried learning from the successful people, but I couldn't compete with all of the brick and mortar companies that were selling their stuff dirt cheap to get it out of their inventory.

The next business that I began was called LLI. I had to sell the program which taught people how to start their own company and then sell tickets to conferences. In the entire six months that I was part of this venture I spent a ton of money and had only sold one $1,000 product. I did learn, however, how to start a company that I was passionate about and how to talk to potential clients on the phone that centered on them and not on me.

My target clients were teachers like myself. They either wanted to leave the school system or were let go from the school system and were looking for a way to make money tutoring online. My company didn't fit their need, so I would always end up wishing them luck as they pursued their future endeavors. This did stick out to me that there was a need, but certainly I couldn't provide that need for them at that time.

So far this whole starting my own business thing was not working out quite like I thought that it would. The fear and frustrations that my husband was having about me not making a reliable income caused some resistance for success to come easily and effortlessly my way. We feared if we would have enough money to pay off our bills and kept going into the negative and into our savings. The money situation wasn't looking good.

Then I remembered the program that I had that taught me how to run my own company. By this point I now was able to create my own websites, do video Marketing and create my own SEO results to get me on page one of Google. I had this brand new idea that I was so excited to implement. This idea would help increase kids reading levels while everyone got to have a good time. I thought I would sell vacations that the entire family could go on. There would be times where mom and dad could spend some alone time together while the kids would be reading about the places that they were at. Then they would have hands on experiences at these exotic locations like Alaska and increase their background knowledge, which would then increase their non-fiction reading levels.

This excited me because I would get to travel the world which was always a passion for me AND I would be able to help kids with their reading. It felt like a win win. The only problem is that there was not a need for this. Nobody goes into Google and types learning vacation. I had people tell me that vacations should be a time where kids get to relax, not learn. Every single negative thought that went through peoples minds about this idea came out of their mouths. Or, so I thought.

In the end, this was not a SERVICE that was going to solve problems for people. Thank goodness this didn't cost me anything. I didn't have to invest anything except for time. So, unfortunately Bright IDEA Vacations where you get to discover, explore and have an adventure was never born.

I had always wanted to teach kids how to read online. Before I had left my first teaching job I had mentioned this to one of my college professors and she had given me this look like I was crazy. She didn't see how I could be effective teaching kids to read online and her look backed that up. I had no idea how to make it work either. So, I began going online to see if there was a company that I could work for.

I found company after company that offered math, SAT, and ACT tutoring. There were companies that seemed to offer language arts tutoring but not tutoring online for struggling readers. I honestly never had a desire to teach those other areas so I left the dream of teaching online for a dream in the future.

I began to think about some other ways that I could make money. I thought that I could take my craft skills and begin making money selling handmade jewelry on Etsy. I didn't sell one piece of jewelry online, so I decided to take my jewelry to a craft fair, get a table and sell it there.

Since there were already a ton of jewelry crafters at the fair I was going to enter, I had to MARKET under a different focus. I made matching jewelry sets for little girls and their American Girl Dolls.

Do you think I was effective at this? Nope, women apparently like to buy jewelry for themselves, but not so much for their little girls and their doll. Also, the day of the fair happened to be on a day where we had a major hail storm and instead of having 1,000 people walk through the door that day, only 200 people attended the event. I had set up my booth so that kids could color while the parents looked around. The only sale I made that day was a pity sale from a little girl that hung out with me coloring.

This was another business venture that landed me into a negative profit. I spent about $300 on beads, $40 on a table and made a whopping $10 from the event. Hmmmm..... I really began to second guess my ability to start a successful business opportunity for myself and continued to brainstorm.

I remember going to an Usborne Book Party once and I loved the books so much that I thought this was something easy that I could be successful at. Anyone who knows me, knows my passion for books, so this seemed like a no-brainer. I attended all of the trainings online, did my research, purchased the start up package and had my open house. I was able to book parties from this and my friends really supported me in this venture.

The problem came when I ran out of friends. My friends were willing to have a party and support me, and even some of their friends supported me, but after that people just didn't want to have parties. It is work for people to bring a sales person to their home to have a party and people don't really want to go through the effort of cleaning their house, inviting their friends, and having someone sell to them. Sometimes the perks where good enough for people to want to do this, but most people didn't really want to invest their hard earned dollars on what seemed to them as expensive but high quality books. Ebooks seem to be really taking off right now and if you can buy a book for .99 or $2.99, then odds are that you are not going to buy them at full price and only read them once.

So there you have it. Five failed businesses and no real potential of earning an income. You may be wondering why I chose to share that story with you. Well, I share it more because of what I have learned in the process of starting my own businesses than to tell you what a failure I have been in the past.

Through each of these businesses I have learned that people don't actually care about the product that you have to sell them. The only thing that people care about is what's in it for them. That is the only thing that will get people to part with their hard earned dollar. So as you are starting your own tutoring business, never think of it as a way to earn money and freedom for yourself, but honestly how can you be of SERVICE to your potential client. Remember that one thing that my mom taught me. "Whatever you do, do your best."

Another powerful thing that I learned through this entire process is that if people's pain is great enough, then they will pay for a solution. The first company that I had with ebay did not result in any pain for people. People can find clothing anywhere. They can go to a rummage sale or goodwill if their pain is great, not pay a lot of money, and still be clothed. The pain factor in your child falling behind in education is great. This is why there is such a need for it.

In my second business I learned that many people want to have financial freedom, but if something sounds too good to be true, they will put their guard up. When I ran my business with Etsy I learned that you can't just put something on the internet anymore and expect people to find it. People don't find things on the internet as an accident anymore. People are found because they have either done their research on SEO to create #1 rankings on Google, have paid for their rankings to show up as #1 and paid a ton of money, or have paid for someone who knows what they are doing in the area of internet Marketing.

The days of people finding you by accident are long over. Everything is very methodical and I will teach you what I have done to get first page rankings. It won't happen overnight, but through time it will be possible. If you want to get started right now I suggest Search Engine Optimization an Hour a Day by Jennifer Capone and Gradiva Couzin. This book will guide you into knowing everything you need to know about optimizing your website about discovering what keywords you need, how to get known for those keywords, and how to get found long term. It is a technical book, but if you follow it step by step you will get found on the internet for free.

I learned that from my venture with Bright IDEA Vacations that sometimes my ideas are not so bright. If you can't laugh at yourself, then who can you laugh at. Don't take yourself so seriously, brush it off, and find another way to turn your dreams into a reality.

I also learned that if my business is more of a benefit to me than it is for my clients, then it will not be an effective business. People are in business because their SERVICES or product is something that other people need, not something I think that they should need or want.

From Usborne Books I learned that I don't enjoy selling low price point products. If someone only buys one, then you don't make much of a profit. I have seen people buy one piece of jewelry from Silpada for $100 and seen both people walk away happy from the transaction. When I would sell my books and someone bought one for $10, only one person walked away happy from that transaction, the customer. This made me take stalk of what ny tutoring company I want my customers

getting great value for their money and I

port my family so that I don't have to go out

pical job.

I have learned from my businesses is this.

_T

- We deserve to get paid for what we are worth for the time that we put in.
- Don't take yourself too seriously.
- Have fun with whatever business venture you decide to be a part of. If it's not fun, then you are not doing it right.
- You can be, do, and have whatever your heart desires.

SYSTEMS

- Always get the training that you need and learn from others when you need it. Effective systems are just at the tip of your finger.
- Don't reinvent the wheel. You will most likely fail unless you have an infinite amount of persistence.
- Learn effective systems from people that are more successful than you.

MARKETING

- People will not find you on accident on the internet.
- Your friends can only take you so far, network and get yourself out there.
- Test your ideas out on others, they will let you know if you have a bright idea.

SERVICES

- Be of SERVICE to others.
- Give the best SERVICE that you can to each of your clients.

This entire book is split up into these specific four categories because I believe this four step system is the key to a successful online business. The Tutorpreneurs program was created specifically to go into details and support online tutors to become successful business owners that have financial freedom, flexibility, and a life beyond their wildest dreams.

4 MINDS

"You won't know the power of
rung of the ladder toward what you w.... ....
the top and find this dream is no longer desirable, you will be
viewing life from a higher vantage point and you will have grown
in you're ability to chase your own dreams." – Troy Fontana

As you can see I didn't go to school to start my own business. It wasn't something that I even had considered before due to beliefs that were instilled in me. In order to go from a typical job to owning my own company I had to go through an incredible MINDSET shift for me. In fact, I don't think any of this would have been possible without the mindset shift. Wayne Dyer wrote a book that goes into depth about the "shift" called, <u>The Shift, Taking your Life from Ambition to Meaning</u>[2].

Growing up during the recession of the 80's taught me that there is no job security in a typical job where you get paid from an employer. At any time, even if you are part of a union, you can get let go. This creates fear, stress, and hard times.

This was all I knew as a child. Since it was all that I knew, I followed in the steps of my family and continued to get job after

---

[2] Dyer, Wayne (2010). The Shift, Taking your Life from Ambition to Meaning. United States, Hay House Inc.

job after job. I didn't know any other way until I began to immerse myself with self development material.

The Secret by Rhonda Byrnes[3] started to get me to think of making money in different ways that would support the lifestyle that I wanted to have. First, I had to figure out what lifestyle that was. I had to figure out what lifestyle I thought I deserved.

In the beginning I thought that as long as I had a house, a family, and a career that I would be happy. Well, I had all of those things and they didn't make me happy. After reading the Secret I began creating what my dream life would look like. Since I was still teaching in the school system, I didn't see how this could be my reality, but I began to believe that I deserved it.

At the same time I also began having a relationship with my Higher Power. I began to receive guidance in what I was meant to do and I began to follow the calling of leaving the school system.

In the book How to Make Great Things Happen in Your Life by Fred Schafer[4] he mentions a study that was done at Yale University in 1959. All of the students were asked to answer a survey at the end of the year. The Survey included the following question.

Do you have a precise written specification – a written focus- of how you want your life to be in 10 years' time? This includes a professional goal, relationship goal, and an overall goal in all areas of your life.

How many students do you think had these kinds of goals exiting one of the top universities in existence? If you guessed 3%, then

---

[3] Byrnes, Rhonda (2006). The Secret. New York: Beyond Words Publishing.

[4] Schafer, Fred (2013). How to Make Great Things Happen in Your Life. Autstralia: Condor Books.

you are correct. However, what I find even more astounding than that is ten years later, every single one of those students was contacted and the results they found were staggering. That 3% that had focused and clear goals had actually achieved more happiness, obtained more tangible goals, created a sense of purpose in life, and accumulated more wealth than the remaining 97%.

People who don't make plans continue on a path of letting life determine their next step and go through the daily grind. Not many people enjoy the daily grind. I know that I didn't. I remember how I felt every Sunday night before I would have to go to work the next day. I would feel sick to my stomach.

Maybe tutoring isn't right for you, maybe it's not your dream. Everyone's dream is going to be different and that is o.k. Do yourself a favor and write down what your 5 year plan and 10 year plan are.

A MINDSET shift has to happen in order for one to go from being an employee to a small business owner. Some people don't want to be a business owner, but what if being a business of a solopreneur company like tutoring let you have freedoms you didn't even know that you wanted. Would you be interested in making the shift?

It is so exciting to not go job from job to job anymore. Imagine having multiple streams of income vs. just one stream of income. Many people have a lot of stress about losing their job, because if they lose their job then they don't know how to pay the bills. Their one source of making money is gone. Now what?

Today I have multiple streams of income coming in. There's tutoring, book sales, product sales, and watching extra kids before and after school. If one of these areas would tank, I wouldn't have to worry about not making money. As each day goes on money flows easily and effortlessly more and more into my bank account. Making money doesn't have to be hard anymore.

This is huge when it comes to MINDSET change. To go from only making money from a job, to having multiple streams of income alleviates the stress involved with losing a job. One can go from a world that is troubled with problems to a world where there is a solution around every corner waiting to be found. Over the next couple of pages you will see some actual activities that you can do to begin making MINDSET changes for yourself. These are not only empowering, but uplifting as well.

Read for an hour a day

Before I even read the book the Secret, by Rhonda Byrnes[5] I did a program called Tools to Life by Coach Devlyn Steele[6]. It is a free online program that has also pivotal in changing my MINDSET.

He gave a powerful suggestion to read everyday for an hour. He challenges us to turn off the television 30 minutes before you go to bed and read instead. The reason is because we tend to listen to the news and it is filled with negative thoughts. If this is going on before we go to bed, then this is what travels through our brain throughout the night and the next day.

On top of reading for 30 minutes before you go to bed, he also suggests reading for an hour a day about things in your specific field. He says that if you do this every day for 3 years, then you will be an expert in your field by the end of that time.

---

[5] Byrnes, Rhonda (2006). The Secret. New York: Beyond Words Publishing.

[6] www.toolstolife.com

For some of us we go through the grind each day, and we don't feel we have the mental capacity to challenge our brains and read. It is so much easier to turn on the television, but honestly once you began doing this, you won't miss television one bit and you will feel like you are being more productive.

Positive Thoughts vs. Negative Thoughts

Did you know that we have 60,000 thoughts that go through our brain every single day? About 80% of those thoughts are negative for most people according to Marci Shimoff[7]. With 48,000 negative thoughts it is really hard to be grateful, but this is part of the mindset change.

In the book 212° the extra degree by S.L. Parker[8], he says this.

At 211 degrees, water is hot.
At 212 degrees, it boils.
And with boiling water, comes steam.
And with steam, you can power a train

Applying one extra degree of temperature to water means the difference between something that is simply very hot and something that generates enough force to power a machine.

The book also mentions that once your negative thoughts are at 49% and your positive thoughts are at 51% that you have reached this extra degree. You are now thinking more positively than negatively and can begin achieving the things that you want to achieve in your life.

---

[7] Women Leading from the Soul Conference March 5, 2013.

[8] Parker, S.L. (2005). 212° the Extra Degree. Flower Mound, TX: The Walk the Talk Company.

Gratitude

Gratitude can be a tool to reach this 51% . Here is the quickest way to begin changing negative thoughts in positive thoughts.

1. Each morning when you wake up write down 5 things that you are grateful for.

2. Each morning before you go to bed write down 5 different things that you are grateful for.

It is easy to fall in a rut of saying the same things over and over again. So, if you make it a point to not repeat ones you have already thought of, you will begin training your brain to look for the positive instead of looking for the negative.

People have said that once they began doing this activity that their thoughts started to focus more on the positive and that they felt more excited to wake up in the morning. Gratitude is a game changer and it is that one degree that can make all of the difference.

Surround Yourself with Top Authors and Motivational Speakers

One thing that you can begin reading are books that begin to change your mindset from those negative thoughts to positive thoughts. A great resource to use is TED Talks online[9]. You will be introduced to amazing motivational speakers who have already had these MINDSET shifts.

---

[9] www.ted.com

Here are some of my favorite authors and the books that they have written.

Rhonda Byrnes – The Secret[10]

Wayne Dyer – Wishes Fulfilled: Mastering the Art of Manifesting[11]

Napoleon Hill – Think and Grow Rich[12]

Stephen Covey- Seven Habits of Highly Effective People[13]

Robert Kiyosaki – Rich Day, Poor Dad: What the Rich Teach their Children and the Poor and Middle Class do not![14]

Eckhart Tolle – The Power of Now[15]

Esther Hicks – The Law of Attraction[16]

Jack Canfield – Chicken Soup for the Soul: Think Positive[17]

---

[10] Byrnes, Rhonda (2006). The Secret. New York: Beyond Words Publishing.

[11] Dyer, Wayne (2012). Wishes Fulfilled: Mastering the Art of Manifesting. New York: Hay House Publishing.

[12] Hill, Napoleon (2009). Think and Grow Rich. United States: White Dog

[13] Covey, Stephen (2012). The Seven Habits of Highly Effective People. New York: Rosetta Books.

[14] Kiyosaki, Robert (1998). Rich Day, Poor Dad: What the Rich Teach their Children and the Poor and Middle Class do not! New York: Warner Books Inc.

[15] Tolle, Eckhart (1999). The Power of Now. Novata, CA: Namaste Publishing.

[16] Hicks, Esther (2006). The Law of Attraction. Carlsbad, CA: Hay House Publishing.

Decluttering

Decluttering your space is an amazing way to begin physically getting rid of the stuff in your life that you don't need, use, or love. So far we have looked at negative thoughts and positive thoughts. Think about how surrounding yourself in things that you don't need or use has the ability to cause negative thoughts.

More stuff means more cleaning and sometimes the stuff can take over. It takes over in the car, in the house, in our office, and everywhere. We know we should take action, but sometimes we spend more time thinking about how much we don't want to do it, that it would actually take less time to actually do it.

I fell into this trap and found an amazing resource called FlyLady[18] online. Fly Lady gave me the tools that I did not have to turn my home into a place that I love. What I have found is that when you surround yourself in things that you love, that you take care of them more. Also, it brings you closer to the most powerful tool according Rhonda Byrnes in The Power[19]. That power is love. When you are in a mode of love you accomplish more and are inspired to take the actions in your life that you feel are necessary to take.

Visualizing

One of the most amazing tools that you can utilize is the tool of visualizing. Visualizing allows you to think big and focus on what you want to attract into your life.

---

[17] Canfield, Jack (2010). Chicken Soup for the Soul: Think Positive. United States: Chicken Soup for the Soul Publishing, LLC.

[18] www.flylady.net

[19] Byrnes, Rhonda (2010). The Power. New York: Atria Books

The key to visualizing is believing what you are visualizing. If you can't believe that you can attract what you are visualizing, then you will not be able to attract it into your life.

Visualizing can be done in several ways. Let's take a look a couple of them.

First, you can visualize by closing your eyes and thinking about what you want to attract into your life. Allow your brain to go free and imagine actually having it. Next, focus on how it feels to have attracted that into your life. When you connect the feeling of love to what you want to attract, you are able to attract it quicker.

Another way to visualize is through using a dream board. You can collect images of the things that you want to attract into your life and put them on the dream board. Each day when you wake up you then focus on it and feel appreciation for attracting these things into your life.

I utilize this same concept on my computer. I take an image and set it as my background image. This allows me to focus on that one really big dream that I want to attract and every single time, the big dreams have always come into my life.

In the next couple of chapters I am going to answer a few questions most people have about running their own online tutoring company so that if this is your dream you can visualize it and think big. Small business owners that think small, don't attract big results. So, let's take a closer look at how successful a tutoring business can be and how much it costs to get started.

5 How successful can a tutoring business be?

"Success is not the key to happiness. Happiness is the key to success. If you love what you are doing, you will be successful."
Herman Cain

When I first began thinking about running my own tutoring business the thought of how successful could this really be went through my mind. The answer to this question is, your tutoring business can be infinitely successful if you change your MINDSET from seeing obstacles as road blocks to seeing obstacles as opportunities.

To be completely honest with you, I didn't know in the beginning that my tutoring business was going to be as successful as it is. In fact, I started off teaching kids to read online for free because I didn't even know if the tools I was putting in place were going to work.

In the beginning I received a lot of resistance from people because for some reason they didn't trust Skype. Honestly you can use whatever two way communication tool where you can both use a webcam that you want. For me Skype was the tool I needed because I was going to be working with very young children. I wanted my students to answer the phone and not have to touch anything else on the computer. Other people may use other tools because they are able to have the other user use the computer. I knew that I would be working with kids as young as 5 years old and in some cases I even work with 4 year olds. So honestly I just need them to follow my lead.

Once I got over the resistance that people had about Skype and was able to show them how easy this was going to be for them, I never had to have the conversation again about why I use Skype. And, I was able to get people to pay me top dollar for my SERVICES. I started off thinking that people might be willing to pay me, a certified reading tutor and reading specialist, at least what people were paying for reading tutoring at other companies. I knew my SERVICES would be more convenient for the average busy family. I found out that parents pay $40 at least an hour for the SERVICES that I provide. So, I started there. Right off the bat I had people willing to pay this because they wouldn't be able to get these SERVICES cheaper anywhere else. Also, their child wouldn't be placed in a small group tutoring situation, but would be receiving top notch one on one SERVICES. I figured that as time went on that I could raise the price as there was a supply and demand situation going on.

I also had leverage when I talked with each of my potential clients because I was able to explain the situation at the tutoring centers and what type of value they would be receiving from me. See, the tutoring companies that are brick and mortar companies have to pay for their building, all of their advertising, and the people that they hire to tutor. The tutor actually only gets paid between $8 and $15 even though the client is paying $40. Wow, that is crazy, right? What credentialed teacher is going to work for that little money? So the people that are actually working for these tutoring companies are straight out of college, people who can't get teaching jobs, or people that are really hard up for money.
I don't know about you, but I think I would entrust my child's education in the hands of the most highly qualified and not the least qualified. My philosophy is that a program doesn't teach a

child an effective teacher that knows how to adapt to a specific child's learning needs teaches a child. What are your thoughts?

I personally work with my students for just one hour a week. Again this is something that you can adapt for what works for you, but I found that two 30 minute sessions a week was a magic formula. The kids didn't have to invest a ton of their time and get bored with a long session and more can actually get accomplished when you are able to split the hour up. Brick and Mortar companies have to do hour sessions to make it feasible. I on the other hand can make it more accommodating to the parents.

What a selling point. The parent does not need to go anywhere to have their child tutored. This means that the parent can do one of the many other things that they need to accomplish such as laundry , dinner, exercise, or sit back and relax for a few minutes. Amazing!

Brick and Mortar companies tend to have kids come in more than once a week. I have even heard of kids that had to come in 5 days a week for a full hour session. Wow, talk about making the kid hate learning. What kid wants to spend their free time doing that. I had one client tell me how she couldn't have her daughter take part in any other activities because they had to drive an hour a day to the sessions and then stay for the hour. There just was no time for anything else. Tutoring online frees people up to put time into education and time developing a well rounded child. Now kids who receive tutoring can take part in sports that once they could only have dreamed of before.

The real question that you may be wondering is whether tutoring online can be profitable to you. We are just going to stick with the $40 number since this is what people are more than willing to pay for your SERVICES. Of course the more specified your niche the more you can charge. We will also stick with the formula of tutoring for an hour a week. If you want to keep your teaching job and just work an extra 10 hours a week, then here is what that would look like.

10 hours x $40 = $400 extra a week = $1,600 extra a month

Wow, so if you work just ten hours a week, then you can make an extra $1,600 a month. What would your life look like if you were able to earn and extra $1,600 a month. Write it down below.

What are some things that you would be able to?

_____

_____

_____

_____

What are some things that you would be able to have?

_____

_____

_____

_____

Where are some places that you would get to travel to?

_____

_____

_____

_____

Let's say that you just want to work during the summer. But, you don't want to work full time because you have had a rough year. You would be happy with working just 20 hours a week. Right?

20 hours x $40 = $800 a week = $3,200 a month = $9,600 for the summer

I am going to pose the same questions as before because I want you to really think of how this can be of value for you.

What are some things that you would be able to?

_____

_____

_____

_____

What are some things that you would be able to have?

_____

_____

_____

_____

Where are some places that you would get to travel?

_____

_____

_____

_____

Let's say that you want to just work part time and take care of your family. Maybe you want to be home for your own kids or maybe you want to watch your grandkids during the day. If you decided that you wanted to work 20 hours a week to have that balance, here is what the numbers would look like.

20 hours x $40 = $800 a week = $3,200 a month = $38,400 a year

So, you could bring in $3,200 a month working part time from your home. Wow, that is amazing. The best part is you can make this and still do what you love to do, which is teach. What part time job can you get where you will work out of your home, not have a boss looking over your shoulder and make $38,400 a year?

What are some things that you would be able to?

_____

_____

_____

_____

What are some things that you would be able to have?

_____

_____

_____

_____

Where are some places that you would get to travel?

_____

_____

_____

_____

Now some of you may be thinking, that just sounds way too good to be true. You may even be one of those people that has been wired to think that if it sounds too good to be true, then it is. I certainly was raised that way. I had to change that MINDSET thought into believing bigger than I was ever able to believe before.

And just to show you that I am not making up these numbers and they are all theoretical, I have been working part time doing this for the last three years. Here is what my PayPal account took in January of 2013 in figure 5.1

figure 5.1

During this month I brought in $3,261.00 and I was only working 11 hours a week.

We started off talking about some pretty small numbers because I wanted you to see how even doing this a few hours a month can impact your income. Now let's take a look at someone who is serious about making this a full time career.

40 hours x $40 = $1,600 a week =$6,400 a month = $76,800 a year

How many teachers do you know that are making $76,000 a year? That is the end of your career salary and you can begin making this today and this is just when you start out. Remember how I mentioned that as there is a supply and demand that you can charge more? Well, let's take a look at how the numbers change as soon as you start charging $50 an hour.

40 hours x $50 = $2,000 a week = $10,000 a month = $120,000 a year

Do you know any classroom teachers that are making this? The answer is no. It doesn't exist. Teachers have never been able to make a 6 figure income and now with starting your own online tutoring company you can and let me tell you, I do all of this without the stress of the administration breathing down my back telling me what to do, when to do it, and how to do it. So, I want you to think bigger than you have ever been able to think before. What would your life look like if you were making $120,000 a year.

What are some things that you would be able to do?

_____

_____

_____

_____

What are some things that you would be able to have?

_____

_____

_____

_____

Where are some places that you would get to travel?

_____

_____

_____

_____

People will pay you what you are worth if you carry yourself professionally and charge a price that is worth your time, then you not only get to be the owner of your life, with the flexibility that you may have always desired, but you also get to be the owner of your very own business. Honestly, what is possible is going to be completely up to you. I will share with you all of the tips and tricks that I use to run my business if you stick with me long enough. You will learn how to do this and find the people that want to hire you for your SERVICES.

6 How much does it cost to run an online tutoring business?

The next question that may be going through your mind, now that you have an idea of what you can earn is how much is running my own tutoring business going to cost me? With the birth of the internet, running an online tutoring business has never been easier. In the past if someone wanted to purchase a franchise and run a tutoring business he/she would have to find a brick and mortar building and pay rent each month.

I went online to find out how much it would cost if you wanted to start a franchise with one of the big tutoring companies. I am going to leave the names of those companies out of this book. This information is only here to put into perspective how easy this all is today.

In order to own a franchise you have to be trained in their programs and pay for the training. Usually there are changes that need to happen to the building in order to effectively run your business and that can cost up to $9,000 just for the architect. The actual improvements can cost between $30,000 and $60,000.

Once the building is secured and renovated to meet your needs you then need to put furniture in the building. That costs anywhere between $10,000 and $20,000. A good computer is also essential and will cost another $800 up to $1,500.

Are you getting tired yet, with all of these numbers and the costs involved. It seems astronomical to me. And I have only hit the tip of the iceberg. Each month you need to pay your payroll to the employees and each month you need to pay about $1,500 in rent. Don't forget about ongoing costs like electricity and water.

I have listed all of the costs in Figure 8:1. The overall cost of running your very own tutoring franchise can be anywhere from $81,243 to $157,750 in the first 3 months. I don't know about you, but I don't even know how to get a hold of that kind of money.

Resources	Low Cost	High Cost
Training Agreement Deposit Fee	$500	$500
Expenses while training	$3,945	5,460
Initial Franchise Fee	$1,000	1,000
Initial purchase of materials	$1,000	1,000
Architect design	$0	9,000
Leasehold improvements	$30,000	60,000
Furniture, signs, equipment & supplies	$10,000	$20,000
Notebook computer at Center	$800	$1,500
Professional fees	1,000	3,000
Liability insurance	$400	$400
Business license, name registration	$100	$200
Lead Management System	$340	$340
Recommended Reading List	$2,240	$2,290
Fingerprinting, criminal background check	$18	$60
Rent	$1,500	$4,000
New center Marketing	2,000	5,000
Payroll cost for assistants	14,400	20,000
Utilities	12,000	24,000
Total	**$81,243**	**$157,750**

Figure 8:1

When I take a look at these numbers I realize how truly lucky I am to have the lifestyle that I have. Never before in history of the world has owning your own tutoring business been easier. Would you like to know the total cost for me to get my business started? $0. I didn't have to invest one penny to get started. I didn't have to pay any money to get trained because I was already a teacher that had a Masters. I didn't have to pay for rent because it was out of my house. I didn't have to pay for Marketing because there are ways to Market for free today and level the playing field for all people. I didn't have to invest in expensive systems because I created all of my own. I never have to pay for architectural design changes because I can use a computer from anywhere in my house. However, later on when I do plan on making changes to my office, it can all be tax deductible. Pretty sweet, right?

That isn't to say that I don't have any costs associated with running my business. Since getting started I have found some tools that are worth investing in to make my life a whole lot easier. I pay $300 a year to have a membership on some websites that are great tools to use with students. I love using PayPal because of how easy it is to get paid and I have set each of my clients up on an automatic payment plan. As of 2013 this currently costs $25 a month + 3% of total sales. These costs are what I consider my assistants. I don't need to hire an assistant because of how easy PayPal has made it for me.

I am a lifelong learner, since I am able to deduct my own professional development on my taxes it is important to mention that I can spend anywhere between $1,000 to $4,000 depending on what my needs are for the year. This may not be something that you see as necessary, but I know that there is always someone out there that has the next piece of information that I need to improve my business or to help me move my business to the next level. I can also justify it because I don't have all of those other sources that I need to spend money on in order to run my business.

I personally believe that it is important to get a business coach if you have never been in business before. I started joining some mastermind forums where we brainstorm answers to business questions that I have. This was the most beneficial investment that I made. There are so many people now at my disposal that if I have a question I can go directly to them and not have to do hours of endless researching on the internet. Having that kind of support is amazing.

I first began thinking about this need to have a business coach while I was watching the Olympics with my daughters. I noticed that every single Olympian had a coach. Not one person was doing it on their own. Then it dawned on me. All successful athletes have coaches, could I make my business more successful by having a coach. I got one and proved that yes, having a business coach can help your business be more successful. Remember, I was coming from the teaching world essentially and had 5 failed businesses. I didn't know what I was doing, so investing in a coach was essential to my success. A coach is able to take a look at where you are and guide you to where you need to be. A coach can also be the go to person when you have business questions.

Table 1 shows each of these costs. The total cost for me in 2012 to have an ongoing tutoring company is $5,180. If I didn't set aside any money for professional development it could cost me just $1,180 a year to run. If you didn't have a business coach it would only be $680 and if you wanted you could even get those costs down and get started just like I did with $0. Not bad. Then on top of everything else I am able to write off business expenses from my total income earned. This is a nice benefit during tax season.

Table 1

Resources	low	high

Membership websites	$0	$300
PayPal	$0	$300
Office supplies	$0	$50
Business cards	$0	$30
Business coach	$0	$500
Personal Development	$0	$4,000
Total	**$0**	**$5,180**

Now that we have taken a look at what it takes financially to run an online tutoring business, let's take a look at what you can write off as a business expense. It is best practice to hire someone the first year that you do your taxes that is familiar with small businesses. But until that time you will be able to save receipts and create an expense report that you will be able to give to the person who will do your taxes.

The first thing that you will want to do is create a file to put in your filing cabinet and simply name it, "Taxes 201_." Every time you purchase something that is listed below you will want to have a place to put your receipt. Inside of your wallet or purse designate a place that you will put receipts so that if you are out and about you can put it there and not have to go searching through an endless pile of receipts later on.

As a business owner you are allowed to write off business expenses that classroom teachers are not allowed to write off. You can keep track of your expenses using a an excel spreadsheet and add to it each month so that when tax time comes it is really easy.

I love to take trips, so I use the acronym TRIPS to help me with what I am allowed to write off as a business expense.

T = Travel
R = Running my business
I = Incur
P = Personal Development

S = Supplies

Travel

The first area that you will be able to make tax write-offs includes all of your travel expenses that are related to your business. You will be able to write off airfare, cabs, and food. All you need to do is hold onto your receipts and put them into your receipts for the current year folder.

When you get home add up the receipts for airfare as one expense, cabs or travel as another expense, and all of the food as another expense. Add up the total, put the information in an excel spreadsheet that is similar to the one listed in table 9:1.

Running your business

Anything that you need to run your business can be written off. Here is a list of items that I am able to write off.

Membership sites

PayPal Merchant Account

Computer

Internet

Phone

Marketing

As an online reading tutor I utilize Raz kids[20] and am able to put this on my expense report and write it off. I also have other membership sites that I am a part of that I can easily write off as well.

You can also write off the expenses for a PayPal Merchant Account. By opening up a PayPal Merchant Account you are able to process credit cards over the phone and have the money go directly into your account. You are also able to create automatic payments from clients on a monthly basis. Both of these things you could not do as of 2012 with a regular PayPal account. It is a SERVICE that will make your life much easier and does not require you to hire someone to be in charge of your payroll.

If you need computer equipment or if your computer equipment breaks down, you are able to write these off. These items include headsets, mouse, actual computer, hard drive, and anything else that is needed in order for you to use your computer to run your business.

Another item that you can write-off is the amount of internet that you use for your business. An example would be if you happened to use 75% of the internet to run your business, then you can take the total amount spent on the internet each month and divide that by 75%. That is the amount that can be tax deductable.

---

[20] www.raz-kids.com

The same is true about the phone. If you have a separate line for your office then you can write that off. Most people run their business using their cell phone. If you used your cell phone 50% of the time for business and 50% of the time for pleasure, then you can write off 50% of your phone bill.

Every penny that you spend on Marketing is a tax write-off. Marketing supplies include flyers, business cards, pay per click advertising, and banner advertising.

In the Home

A percentage of your house can even be tax deductable. If this is something that you wish to do, you definitely want to talk to the person doing your taxes and decide if this is a good decision for you.

If you have 2000 square foot home and 10% of that home is taken up by your office, then you can deduct that amount of your mortgage payment. You can even deduct 10% of electricity since you need that to run your business. If you think about it, if you had a brick and mortar business, then you would have to pay these expenses. The government does not treat a brick and mortar small business much different than a home business.

Some people who run a home business have a hard time being on top of cleaning their house and running their business. These people hire a cleaning company to come in and help. This is another business expense that can be deducted based on the percentage of your office to your home.

Not everything in your home is tax deductible and each state has it's own laws. If you are in another country you will have to check with the laws of your country. This is why I highly suggest getting a tax accountant the first year to make sure that you are taking advantage of every benefit that you possibly can.

Professional Development

There is always information to learn out there. Whether you are learning more about owning your own business or getting professional development in the specific area that you are teaching online, you can write it off. Here are some examples.

Conferences
Books
Professional organizations
Professional magazines
Professional Membership Sites
Networking groups

Any conferences that you attend can be a write off. I usually attend the Wisconsin State Reading Association conference, International Reading Association Conference, Homeschooling conferences, and Marketing conferences. All of these can be written off as a business expense.

Often when I hear about a book that contains the information that I need to grow my business or do something better, I go on Amazon and purchase it. Not only is it cheaper on Amazon, it is amazingly convenient. You can simply print a copy of your receipt, mark it in your expense report and put it in a file where you save a hard copy of all of your receipts.

I am a member of the International Reading Association and not only is my membership to the organization a write off, but so are the monthly magazines that keep me on top of best practices.

I am a part of some online communities that are membership sites and even the online community that I run, The International Association of Online Tutors, is tax deductible for all of it's members.

You may wonder why you would pay to be a part of a community online. The answer is simple, it weeds out those people on the internet that are trying to Market to you vs. add value to what you want to accomplish in your business.

When you own your own business it is a good idea to join some different networking groups. You certainly can go to Meetup to join some. You can also join professional networking groups. These groups consist of professionals and they exist because people want to network and help each other out. I received one of my best clients from a networking group and it has proven to be well worth the money that I invested.

Supplies

Lastly you can write off any supplies that you need to run your business. Here is a list of some of the supplies that I utilize.

1. Notebooks
2. Binders
3. Staples
4. Paperclips
5. Tape
6. Folders
7. Pens
8. Pencils
9. Pencil Sharpener
10. Computer Paper
11. Ink for printer

Pretty much any office supply that you need can be written off. Some of these may seem like tiny things to worry about, but some of them are more expensive like printer ink. It all adds up, so it doesn't hurt to jot them down.

Table 2 shows what an excel spreadsheet that is used as an expense report could look like.

Conclusion

Seventy percent of the amount of tax deductions that home based businesses can deduct completely get left off each year. Don't be part of that 70%. Take all of the advantages that you can. You will be required to pay your own health and save your own money for retirement, so these deductions can help when it comes to those things.

Table 2

Expenses	Jan.	Feb.	March	April	May	Nov.	Dec.	Year
Travel								
airfare								
transportation								
food								
Running your business								
Membership sites								
PayPal								
Computer								
Internet								
phone								
Marketing								
In the Home								
Electricity								
Mortage								
Professional Development								
Conferences								
Books								
Professional Organizations								
Professional magazines								
Professional Membership sites								
Networking								
Supplies								
office supplies (pens, pencils)								
computer paper								
printer ink								
Total								

STEP 2
ORGANIZED SYSTEMS

Organized systems are those systems that need to be in place in order for you business to operate easily and efficiently. The systems that are discussed in this section will give you a look at what needs to be in place. You will begin to learn about keeping track of your records for tax deductions, creating a business plan, and life saving online tools.

7 Figuring out your Niche and your Ideal Client for your Business Plan

When it comes to organization, every successful company needs to start with a business plan. In my Tutorpreneur[21] course I walk people step by step into creating a successful business plan so that they can figure out their mission, vision, and specific goals.

In this chapter we are going to take a look at one part of the business plan that will guide you as you think about the SERVICEs you want to provide and how to market them.

First let's take a look at a niche. What is a niche? A niche is a an area that you would consider yourself an expert at. An example would be teaching reading, math, or SAT Prep.

The ideal client is a person that you want to specifically tailor your tutoring to. You are going to want to get clear about what you

---

[21] To learn more about the Tutorpreneur course sign up to receive free videos to grow your business and more details will be shared with you.
www.tutorpreneurs.com/free-videos

want to tutor and who you want to teach to. The more clear that you can get, the better your advertising will be.

Some people want to teach everything to everyone. I tell people to keep their guard up for people like this because people who think that they are great at everything are usually not very good. You have the whole world at your disposal, so you don't have to ever worry about their not being enough clients out there for you.

Answer the following questions to get clear about your business.

1. What do you want to teach online?

   _____

   _____

   _____

2. Why should people come to you to teach it to them?

   _____

   _____

   _____

3. Who else is already good at what you want to do online?

   _____

   _____

   _____

4. What age range are your students?

   _____

   _____

   _____

5. Who is your ideal client?

   _____

   _____

_____
_____
_____
_____
_____
_____
_____
_____
_____
_____
_____
_____
_____
_____
_____
_____
_____
_____
_____
_____

You may have noticed that I have given you a ton of space to figure out who your ideal client is. The reason is because this allows you to target your advertising in a specific manner that makes people feel like you are talking to them personally. You will be more apt to attract your ideal client than if you don't do this exercise.

When I first figured out who my ideal client was it looked like this.

Marissa is 34 years old and she has graduated from college. She is going back to school herself for her MBA while working full-time at Kohl's corporate and taking care of her two kids Melissa and Joey. She desperately wants school to be easy for her kids and not have to struggle like she did. She wants the best for them and their education.

Marissa is married, but her husband travels a lot, so many of the responsibilities fall on her when it comes to taking care of the home and her children. She wishes she could have more quality time with her kids, but with soccer practice, swim, school, and taking care of the house there just isn't a lot of time.

Marissa sits down with Melissa every night to do homework, but Melissa is not open to mom helping. She frequently tells her mom that she is wrong and that she wishes dad were home to help her. This frustrates Marissa. Marissa doesn't understand why reading is so hard for her child. Even though she struggled through school, reading just seemed to come easy for her. She is lost in how to help her daughter and is looking for resources that she can tap into.

Marissa absolutely hates her job, which is why she is going back to school, but she knows she has to keep her job to help support her family. She is willing to do everything for her family, even stay in a job that she does not care for. Her job and Melissa's struggles with school keep her up at night. When she is frustrated she comes to my blog to see if there are any other tips and tricks that she can utilize with her daughter to make reading fun and not feel like a chore.

Marissa values education and is willing to go to any lengths to ensure that her own kids have a good education. When the kids go to bed, Marissa looks for ideas that she can implement to make sure that she is raising readers.

You may have noticed that I have given my ideal client a name. There are robots out there on the internet, but the people that you want to attract are real people and they have a set of real problems. What are those problems for your ideal client. What is your ideal client looking for from you and why would your ideal client benefit from your SERVICES. Remember that you are in this business to be of SERVICE and to give the best SERVICES that you can to a specific group of people. The more targeted you get, the more people who will have the opportunity to find you. Even people that you are not targeting will find you. Then you are left with the tough decision of whether you will choose to work with them or not.

When I create my videos I create them for this client. When I post messages on Facebook, I picture Marissa and speak right to her. When I create flyers, I keep her in mind so that she can find me. I give specific advice to her on my blog and tweet tips to her during the day. I owe it to Marissa for her to find me. She is looking for the SERVICES that I provide and it is my duty to not let her down. My laziness could result in her child suffering even more.

Notice how I only focus on reading and how my ideal client is looking specifically for help with her daughter's reading. This clarity allows me to focus on one area and to learn everything I need to learn in order to stand out as one of the best. If you are competing against the world, can you really afford to skip this step? I think not.

If you have left the ideal client space blank, then go back and fill it out. This is a critical step in your advertising and in attracting the people that you want to help. Skipping this step is not an option to those who seek success.

8 Favorite Online Organizational tools you can't live without

Remember when Oprah used to have her show called her "Favorite Things" at Christmas time? Well, that is kind of like this chapter in this book. It is all about my favorite tools that I use to run my online tutoring business. Some of the tools are cheap and some of them are free, but these are tools that I use to run my business that I could not live without.

LastPass

The first tool that I use is called LastPass. Have you ever been frustrated at the amount of passwords that you have to remember? Well, I can't seem to remember any of them. I read about what Last Pass could do for me and my life changed from that moment on.

With LastPass I only have to remember 1 password. Lastpass keeps track of all of the passwords and automatically logs me in when I go to websites that require logins. I love it. I can access Lastpass on any computer, so no longer do I need to keep a list of my passwords or try a billion different combinations to get into the different websites.

Lastpass is has two options. One is a paid option and one is free option. I have never needed to move to the paid option, so the free option for now for me is perfect. Not only is this a great tool for running my business in my home, but it is phenomenal when I am somewhere else in the world, working on a different computer. All I do is go to Last Pass[22], sign in and all of my sites are right there. If I can't remember how to get access to one, then I put it in the search bar, it comes up, and once I click on it you can get instant access without ever having to put the information in. The only password you will ever need again is your Lastpass password.

Skype

Skype has given me financial freedom. I know that most people are familiar with it now, but when I got started not only had people not heard about it, some were scared of it. I found this quite funny, but this was a real fear for people.

You may encounter people who have this fear regarding Skype and I am going to share with you the ones that I heard so that you can reassure people of their safety with this amazing tool.

Back in 2010 when I told my sister-in-law what I wanted to try with teaching kids online using Skype, and helping out her son for free, she was nervous because she had to put some personal information like her telephone number to get the account. Some people have a real fear of their information being anywhere on the internet. I reassured her that this was something that Skype needed to do to verify that she was a real person and not a robot.

I have had people ask me why I specifically choose Skype to use

---

[22] www.lastpass.com

and not another program. For me, there were two basic selling tools. It is not only free for me, but also for the client. Also, I am able to share my screen and the child doesn't have to do a thing. In fact the parent can even take the keyboard away from the child and the child will still have the same quality session as if she had the keyboard.

I often hear from people that working with Skype is a completely impersonal experience. The people that share this opinion have never been on Skype for the most part, so don't take it personally if someone says this to you. It is completely personal if you are a personable person. If you have social skill problems with people in everyday life, then you are going to have social skill problems with people you are working with on the computer. I am a completely personable person and I have been told time and time again that my authenticity comes through loud and clear on the other side. My students and I joke around during our sessions and honestly have a great time. The one thing that I would have to say that I miss is having the ability to give my students a great big hug because they are so sweet. So I have invented the virtual hug, which is definitely not as good as real one.

If you are one of those people that is afraid of Skype and you have never used it, give it shot. My thought is that you will learn to love it pretty quickly. It is not a perfect system, but I haven't found a better one out there for what I do. I have tried Go to Meeting, Google, and other classroom formats that haven't matched up to what Skype can do for me and my students.

I highly suggest that you check around and see what is going to work for you and your business. It doesn't hurt and most companies are willing to give you a 30 day free trial test drive.

Dropbox

Before the discovery of Dropbox the only way that I could teach lessons to my students on a different computer was to have a USB. I soon found out that not all of my files would open and I was left having to come up with a new lesson plan.

With the discovery of Dropbox I am able to log into www.dropbox.com from anywhere in the world and immediately access all of my files that are in it for free. If you ever need extra space in your folder you can invite some friends to try it or pay a $9.99 fee for 100 GB of space.

Now I can access everything easily and effortlessly. It truly is amazing. I also utilize Google Drive, but have found Dropbox better for storing my tools I use with each of my students. Google Drive is a great resource to use if I need to share files with someone else. I can share a link with the person and they can view it within their Google drive. If you have a big file you no longer have to worry about it not downloading and being able to be sent to the person that needs to receive it.

PayPal

It seems like everyone is accepting PayPal as a payment option and it has allowed me to take payment, send out invoices, and create automatic payments. Because of PayPal I only need to focus on billing and finances for an hour a week. This means that I am able to run my business without having to pay someone to take care of this part.

PayPal is a safe place that people can pay you and not have fear about what is happening to their money. PayPal uses data encryption technologies, and secure servers that are connected to the internet. They also have a team of anti-fraud experts that protect you as the seller of your SERVICEs and your client.

Also, PayPal stores all of the information that you need regarding payments you have received so that you have access to that information whenever you need it. I usually refer to it when I am doing my taxes to double check. Also, I use it when I track how much I have made each month. PayPal takes care of all the calculations so that I do not have to.

PayPal does charge a fee for each transaction and takes a percentage just like a credit card company would do. As of 2013, each transaction costs .30 and PayPal takes 2.9% of the total paid to you.

PayPal also makes it possible for you to sell internationally and have international clients. This really takes all of the hassle out of it for you. When my Australian clients pay me, neither of us have to figure out exchange rates. This is all taken care of by PayPal.

YouTube

YouTube has provided my business with not only an online presence, that I have over 1,000 subscribers to, but it also gets found in Google on page 1 without spending any money 53x quicker than without it. Wow, that is a pretty staggering statistic., just storing my videos there. In fact, I had created a video, but hadn't actually done my keyword work yet. I was just getting the information out there and was going to figure that out later. BTW, I will cover keywords and how to get found without having to pay a dime in chapter 12. So I began doing the research for my keywords and found one keyword that was so good and was bound to get me amazing results that I edited the video title with the keyword and within 5 minutes I was on page one for that keyword. People spend a ton of money to get these results and I was able to get them immediately because of YouTube. Now that is power.

YouTube is what I would consider the 500 pound gorilla for video Marketing. In fact, it is the second biggest search engine in the world. So, if you want to get found to tutor kids or adults online, you need to be on YouTube. If you don't, then you are throwing thousands of dollars in possible income down the drain.

The world is so great now. I have never been more excited about technology is than where it is today. So, I already know that some of you reading this book are thinking, there is no way I am going to get on a camera. No worries, you don't have to. You can create a ton of videos for free using VideoScribe. All you need to do is go to www.sparkol.com to access it. This program will allow you to try it free for 7 days. At which time you can create a ton of great videos and have them at your disposal on YouTube or wherever else you decide to use them.

Wufoo

An amazing organizational tool that I use to collect information from my clients is called wufoo.com. With this tool you have the ability to create 3 forms for free.

Before setting up an appointment with a client you can collect information that will make it easy for you to have all of the information that you need. An example is included in figure 1.

Information that you will want to collect are not only the child's name that you are assessing, but also a space for a second child if the parent has you working with more than one of their kids.

Often times parents want you to work with more than one child and in Wufoo you cannot have them fill out two separate forms. So this has all of the information that you need in one place. Also, it is less cumbersome for the parent to have to fill out the same for two times.

It is helpful to have the child's address so that you know what time zone the child is in. Also, if you want to send birthday cards or Christmas cards, then you will have the information that you need without having to ask the client for that information.

Sometimes parent will contact you using a different e-mail than the one they originally used, so by having him/her fill this out on the registration form you are asking them which e-mail is the best one to contact you at.

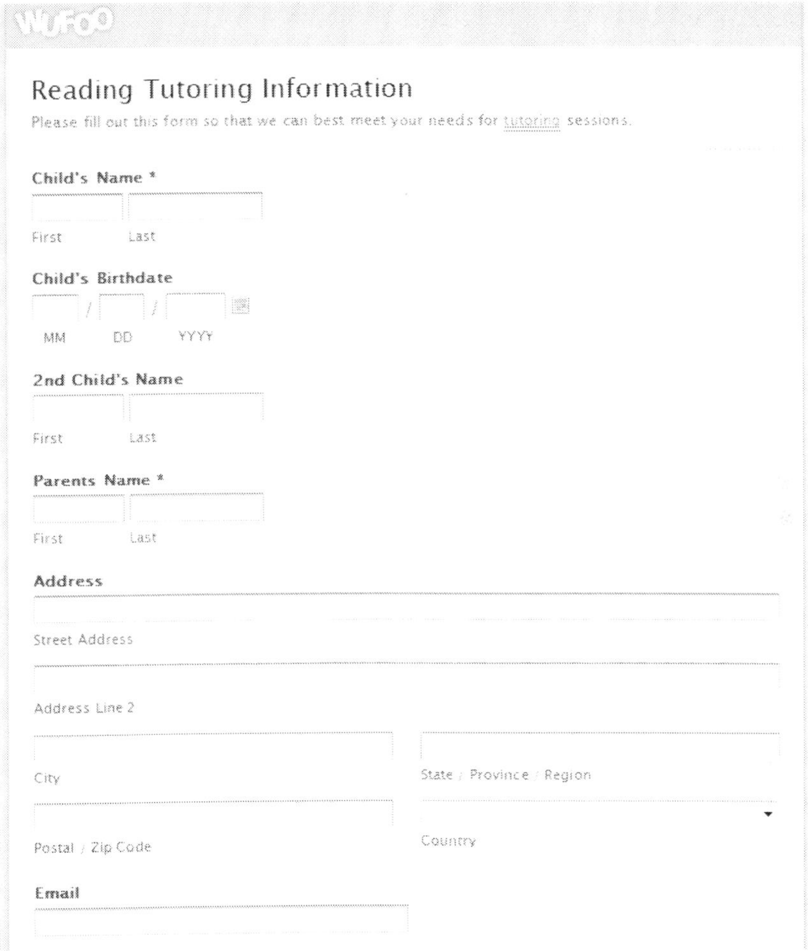

Wufoo

Reading Tutoring Information

Please fill out this form so that we can best meet your needs for tutoring sessions.

Child's Name *

First Last

Child's Birthdate

MM / DD / YYYY

2nd Child's Name

First Last

Parents Name *

First Last

Address

Street Address

Address Line 2

City

State / Province / Region

Postal / Zip Code

Country

Email

Figure 1

Figure 2 is a continuation of the same form. It is important to collect the phone number in case the child does not show up to a scheduled appointment. Then you will have the ability to call and make sure that everything is going o.k. with the technology. Sometimes people just forget and other times they are having computer problems. It is always nice to give them a call and see if there is anything that you can do to help out.

The next section has a place where you can have the parent write down information in regards to what the child is struggling with.

Since I teach reading, I have the parent share information about the child's reading up to this point.

The Next set of information is critical. It is helpful to have what days will work with their schedule and the times that will work. This way you can simply take a look at what fits into your schedule and once the assessment is set up you can start figuring out days and times that will work. After an assessment it is pivotal to set up a time to begin working with the child. Most parents want to start right away.

Phone Number

[____] – [____] – [____]

####

Tell us about your child's reading experiences up to this point.

Check the days that work best for tutoring

☐ Monday
☐ Tuesday
☐ Wednesday
☐ Thursday
☐ Friday
☐ Saturday
☐ Sunday

Select times that work best for reading tutoring

☐ 8am –9	☐ 9am –10	☐ 10am – 11
☐ 11am – 12	☐ 12pm – 1	☐ 1pm – 2
☐ 2pm – 3	☐ 4pm –5	☐ 5pm –6
☐ 6pm –7	☐ 7pm –8	☐ 8pm –9

[Submit]

Figure 2

Now that you have collected all of the information that you need, you can take that form and copy it into a word document and save it to the child's folder you create on the computer. Print off the form and staple it into a manila folder that you will use to keep track of the child's information.

Communities

The online communities that I am a part of have always been lifesavers. Whenever I have a question about something I know where I can go. I don't have to spend endless hours of research trying to figure something out. I can put my question out to the community, walk away for a couple of hours, and have several answers by the time I come back. That is time management at it's best.

There are groups that are free like LinkedIn and Facebook. There are also paid communities.

I personally have a community that I have been building online that specifically helps people just getting started with their company called The International Association of Online Tutors. We answer those questions that you need answers to and support and encourage each other every step of the way. I will share with you at the end of the book how you can get access to that community.

When I started tutoring online I felt like I had to do everything the hard way. There was not really anyone that I could contact and ask for help like I could when I was in the school system. I tried to find people like me that were doing what I was doing and made some contacts, but they weren't quality contacts. I tried asking questions and being as helpful as I could in return, but it was really hard. So I had to learn everything by trial and error. I seriously want to save you time and money so that it doesn't have to take you three years to finally have the systems in place that are going to make your job easy and effortless.

We are all in this together and will support each other in such amazing ways. I don't tutor everything to everyone, so one thing that I like to do is suggest another great tutor in the online world that can support my clients. I do this free of charge, because people do this for me on a daily basis. What would a community of people like that for you and your business be worth to you? For me, it is priceless.

The community is also a place to come to share things that maybe aren't working and get suggestions from people that have been doing the things that you have been doing. The community organizers can even personally walk you through some of the areas that are difficult for you or create a video that you can view at your leisure. Talk about support.

STEP 3
MARKETING

9 Where will I ever get my students from

Are you wondering where you will ever get enough clients to make the income that you desire? Do not worry, remember to keep your focus on the things that you do want and they will come easily and efficiently for you. This chapter is going to begin to touch on some of the marketing tools to make sure you always have the amount of clients that you desire.

First you want to let everyone know what you are currently doing now as an online tutor. Fifty percent of my clients are people that I know or have met personally. The other 50% come from the internet and referrals.

Referrals

When I was doing Usbourne books I had a tough time getting people to book a party. I had to have a lot of free stuff in order to entice them that this was going to be a good move for them. If you have ever been involved in a direct sales company like this then you know what I am talking about.

Your tutoring business is going to be nothing like that. People love giving referrals of great SERVICES. You won't even have to ask them to do it. People love referring great people.

When someone refers a client to me the client never feels that their friend is only referring them because they are going to get something out of it. They are referring the SERVICE because they genuinely care about the educational success of their child. Pretty awesome right? Everyone leaves that conversation feeling like a winner. The person who referred feels great because they know they are passing on a great name and a great SERVICE to their friend. The person getting the referral feels like they are in great hands before they even start working with the tutor.

This past summer I had another parent refer my SERVICES because she knew what I did. I have 3 little girls and her girls are in the same classes as mine. She wasn't sure if I was actually good at what I did, but she knew that I had this tutoring company online and that I specifically focused on reading. So, she gave the woman my website and passed the information along. This woman contacted me, I gave her daughter a free assessment, free report, and first session for free. Before the free trial was done, she had mentioned that she had already started to see results. After three months of tutoring with her daughter in reading her daughter went from being at the bottom of her class at the end of first grade to the top of her class beginning second grade. Her daughter increased her reading level 3 full grades with just 12 hours of instruction.

So this parent was obviously happy about those results and went back to her friend. She said, "Wow, you really know great people." See how this was a win-win for everyone? I did nothing except make sure that people knew what I did.

You may be wondering about some of the tactics that have been successful to get the word out. First, I always have business cards. My favorite resource is Vistaprint[23]. They will make you a ton of business cards cheap. I purchased the higher end cards that were

---

[23] www.vistaprint.com

glossy and received 250 cards for $30. They even have free business cards that you can get and all you pay is for the shipping and handling. The truth is people want your business card, so make sure you have what the people want. You will feel silly when someone asks you for you one and you don't have one. Some people want more than one because they want to just give it to their friends and not have to write anything down on a piece of paper for them. The people in your circle are going to be proud of you and support your endeavors, allow them to help you out.

Siblings

I often have one family have me work with more than one of their children. I have worked with several twins, brothers, sisters, cousins, and so on and so forth. I have even had people have me stop working with one of their kids because their child was doing so well and then have me begin working with another child.

This is when you know that the SERVICES that you are providing are worthwhile to others. When parents don't want to give you up because you are so good and they keep coming up with ways that they can utilize your SERVICES.

I never advertise that I work with kids in math, but for students, past students, or siblings I will. I have found that if a child is struggling with reading and then they are struggling with math, it is usually because of vocabulary and word problems. Those are my two favorite areas to tackle. The methods that I utilize focus on teaching the essential reading skills needed in order to be successful with math.

E-mail

Another awesome resource that I use is called WiseStamp[24] in my e-mail. With Wisestamp I am able to create an extremely professional e-mail signature. My e-mail signature has a picture of me, which is my trademark, the title of my company The Skyping Reading Tutor, my website, ways to find me on Facebook, Twitter, LinkedIn, Pinterest, and Wordpress. As a part of my signature I have the latest blog post, which always deals with reading or tutoring and my skype ID.

Anyone who clicks on those tabs will see my social media presence and anyone that I send an e-mail to can find me and see what I do. It is amazing how just having this one tool actually gives me free promotion of my SERVICES. I am the room mom for my 6 year old and 10 year old. The president of the PTO e-mailed all of the parents to put together a basket for a fundraiser to expand the library at my daughter's school. When I told her that I would put together a basket and get back to her by the end of the day she asked if I did reading tutoring. I explained my business very briefly and she said, "Why don't you make a basket that revolves around your company?" She said that she would put business cards by the basket for any potential customers and get the word out there about what I do.

Wow, this was all because of using WiseStamp and having my information on my e-mail signature. I honestly don't think that I would have used this opportunity to self-promote myself. I usually just see myself as a person that likes to be of SERVICE. So, I got my name out there to a high end clientele about my SERVICES for free. I didn't have to put any effort into it besides putting together a basket, that I already had to put together as

---

[24] www.wisestamp.com

the room mom. In the basket I included a free coupon for SERVICES, some books that I have written and autographed, and some school supplies. Here is a picture of the basket.

So I could get another client out of this and an unlimited amout of leads. That is a win-win for everyone. As you have probably noticed, I like win-wins.

LinkedIn

If you are not on LinkedIn yet, then get on LinkedIn. Here is the big reason why. LinkedIn is a professional website that is going to show your clients how good you really are. Your experience working as a teacher will be here to begin building credibility. There is a feature that is called endorsements that you can use to get known in your field. Because of all of the endorsements that people have given me I received an e-mail from LinkedIn that I am in the top 1% most recommended person for tutoring. The best part is, I didn't do anything to get that. I just listed the areas that are my expertise and people that I am connected with began endorsing me. I didn't even ask them to do that. LinkedIn actually sent them all of the information and gave them the tools to endorse me. The secret to LinkedIn is to make sure you fill out your information at 100%. LinkedIn will be your best friend if you do and you will be the top person to get found in your niche.

Also, I ask all of my clients that if they have liked the work that I have done to please write a recommendation on my LinkedIn page. What I like about this tool is that people can't fake good SERVICE on LinkedIn. People know that testimonials on a website could be fake, but you can't fake a great testimonial on LinkedIn. If you have recommendation after recommendation on this site, then people will automatically begin to see you as an expert in your field.

Blog

Instead of a website you might want to consider doing a blog. Google will find you easier if you have content that you are currently putting on the web vs. a static website. Do you know how many websites are placed on the internet each day? A ton. Remember what I said before, people will not find you by accident, so you will want to be strategic.

You might be thinking that you have never started a blog before and that you don't have the slightest clue where to start with that. No worries, a person that I highly recommend, Michelle Shaeffer, will guide you step by step. Just go to http://michelleshaeffer.com/. She has been one of my business coach's and the amount of information that this amazing woman has inspires me on a daily basis.

Facebook

If you are already on Facebook, then it will be easy to just start telling people what you are doing with your tutoring business. You can post updates with how it is all going for you and how excited you are. Your friends will want to promote you, so let them.

You will want to create a business page on Facebook and invite all of your friends to like you. This again will show credibility so that when others look you up you don't look like a loner in cyber world.

Recently, I was going to do business with a guy who claims to be a specialist in a certain area. When I went to his page that would support he is a specialist in this area I noticed that he had an extremely small crowd. Don't be like that guy. Get yourself out there on the internet because if you are running an online tutoring company people want to see a social media presence that is strong, not weak. I will trust you more if you have more of a following. If you have a small following people may put their guard up and not trust you and this can lead to a loss in business.

Craigslist

Every couple of months I put an ad out on Craigslist for free. I only target my local area because that is how Craigslist is designed. Some people try to advertise on all of the Craigslist sites, but I find that is sneaky and Craigslist does too. In fact, Craigslist will remove your ad if you decide to do that. So if you offer in home tutoring as well with your online tutoring program you can mention that.

When you are filling out the craigslist form all you need to do is check the category *SERVICES offered* and then a new screen will come up and you will select *lessons and tutoring*. From here you will need to write up a description of your SERVICE.

A sample Craigslist ad could look something like this.

Is your child struggling with reading and you wish you could find a way to make it easy for him/her? Joanne has 12 years experience with teaching kids to read. In fact she is able to close the gap a full year with just 8-12 hours of instruction. Check out her website at www.theskypingreadingtutor.com or call 123-456-7890. A couple of times have just opened up, but they go fast so call Joanne soon.

Since you are able to include a picture I personally like to upload a picture of myself. I have one where I am smiling. Here is an example that I have included.

Also people can see exactly where you are located because they have it set up with maps. This adds to the trust value for your potential client. Ultimately, the more information that you give people online, the more that they will trust you. Some people have a fear of putting their information on the computer like their address and phone number. If you are one of those people, then this is probably not a good career path for you. The more people can find out about you online, the more they will trust you.

YouTube

My favorite type of advertising is to make videos. I personally like making videos and playing with my keywords because I can get found very easily this way. In fact, if you type in reading tutor and click on videos on Google, you will find one of mine on the first page. People these days don't look past the first page much. They figure that the best information is either on the 1st, 2nd, or 3rd page. If what the person is looking for is not on one of those pages, then they usually just try another search. So first page ratings is going to be pivotal to your business.

You might think, well I don't like being on camera. No worries. You can make videos easily without having to have your face on the camera. I have made a ton of them. If you go to www.tutorpreneurs.com/free-videos and sign up I will send you 10 videos that will help further your business. You will notice in these videos that I use a program called videoscribe[25]. This SERVICE has a free trial period of 7 days. From there it only costs $19.99 a month and you can make all of your videos in one month and cancel if you wish.

Another way to make a video is to do a screencast. In a screencast you can have the camera on the screen and just record your voice. You provide helpful content to people looking for you and make yourself stand out as an expert without having to put your face on the camera.

Today it is easy to edit your videos. I use the software that comes on my computer, which is Windows movie maker. I also use my iphone and ipad. If you went to www.tutorpreneurs.com/free-videos you will see that I just used my iphone and imovie (an app on my iphone). I recorded the video in 2 minutes and spent about 10 minutes editing it. The part that took me the longest was waiting for it to upload to YouTube.

Making videos can really be that easy. If you combine one of your videos with a blog post Google will reward you even more as long as you are entering the keywords properly.

Paid Advertising

So far I have only mentioned some of the ways that you can get free advertising. I have only hit the tip of the iceberg with free methods, but I wanted to put out there that if you do want to pay for advertising, there are a ton of opportunities to do that as well. If you want to start off with a ton of new customers you can give it a shot. I haven't had to do this for this business because all of the other methods I have utilized have worked so well.

If paid advertising appeals to you then you will want to check out

---

[25] http://www.sparkol.com

Google and Facebook. You can target the market that you would like to tutor this way and get some pretty good results. If you don't know what you are doing though, find someone who does because pay per click advertising can get expensive quickly.

The way that advertising works for Google and Facebook is that you decide how much money you will spend in a day. Let's say that you would like to spend $20. People then put bids on keywords and Google will let you know how much it will cost you every time someone clicks on your ad. Each click can range from .20 to $3 on average. So, you don't really get a lot of bang for your buck with this. Facebook also does paid advertising in a similar manner.

Certain websites have it set up that you can purchase space on their site. Typically you can purchase banner ads or smaller ads and pay a fee for a month.

You can also do some typical advertising through newspapers or magazines if you wish. Again, this is a more expensive method to utilize, but you can rationalize it if you take into consideration that just one customer is going to bring you $160 to $400 a month. Also, waiting rooms and doctor's offices tend to hold onto to old copies of magazines, so your advertisement could be around for a while.

10 Building Trust with Potential Online Clients

We owe it to our potential clients to show the most authentic side of ourselves online as we can. People have their guard up when they are online. They believe that there are two different worlds out there. There is the world that we live in where we can see everyone's faults and weaknesses and then there is the online world where people can make themselves seem like they are something that they are not.

At this point in time anyone can be an online tutor. There are no restrictions out there and this is a position that people do not need to have credentials for.

Those of us that do have credentials want to use that to our advantage. You will set yourself up as an expert if people can go on LinkedIn and see what your experience has been with teaching, what your credentials are educationally, and look at your endorsements and recommendations.

People who think that all they need to do is put a website up to start their business and just tell people about their company are very sadly mistaken. You need to begin to build a relationship with people online, not just tell them what you do for your own benefit and never interact with them.

There is a great book out there called Engagement from Scratch[26] by some of the top authors that have built phenomenal communitites and trust online. Dany Iny is the author and co-founder of Firepole Marketing. If you want to interact with people in a meaningful manner online, then you have to get a copy of his book.

You will find that people will friend you and never introduce themselves to you on Facebook. So the question that automatically comes to my mind is, "Why do they want to friend me? Do they want to spy on me? Do they want to just make it look like they have a lot of friends, or do they want to sell me something?"

This is not a great way to build up trust is it? Seriously, people are not clear online and for whatever reason people feel more important if they have 1,000 friends on facebook rather than 200. Some people friend only people that they know and try to lock and secure their facebook world. I am pretty nice and will friend everyone who wants to be friends. If people are trying to sell me something and aren't really interested in being what I would call a "friend," or they are constantly sending me Marketing messages, then I just defriend them.

I allow people to watch me online and find out as much as they can because I am secure in who I am and what people will see me doing online. I am not afraid to have an online presence because a large part of what I do is online. Remember that 50% of my clients find me online, so if they feel more comfortable sitting in the back row and watching me for a little while, I am o.k. with that.

I think that it is important to get to know the differences between some of the social media out there. Facebook and Twitter are

---

[26] Iny, Dany (2011). Engagement from Scratch. Available on Amazon

comparable to places like the grocery Market and my kids school events. I can be casual, laid back, and just share in the glory of life with them. LinkedIn is my professional background. I consider this the new age resume. I pretty much only put information on there that is about my business, successes that I have had, and allow other people to put all of their endorsements and recommendations about me on there. I don't share information about my kids soccer game, that is information that I share on Facebook.

Also, in LinkedIn there are groups that you can join. I join parenting groups, online teaching groups, and things that relate to my business here. I am allowed to join 40 groups, so I have made sure to do that. I can interact and engage with people and in each of these groups there is an area called promotion. When I put my kindle books for free or when I have spots open for online reading tutoring, then I can put this information in there and people who are interested can take a look at it. It is a win-win for everyone.

Since the release of this book we have started a new group on LinkedIn called The International Association of Online Tutors. This is another place outside of the paid community for people to come together and help each other out. Come on by and say hi.

Another way to gain trust of your online clients is to always be prompt. If you give people a time to meet on Skype, make sure to be there when you say you will be there. If you are late even just a couple of times, you could lose a client.

The most important thing is to be authentic and be who you are in the real world. If you wouldn't say something to someone's face, then don't say it online. Also, no one is attracted to people that complain all of the time online or are having back and forth arguments with people. Always put your professional side forward and so that people can be genuinely attracted to you.

11 testimonials

Testimonials seem to be everywhere and they are one of the most important marketing tools that you will have at your disposal. If you check out other successful businesses you will find they have testimonials. In this chapter we are going to delve into why you need testimonials, how to get testimonials, and where to put testimonials. I will share the different versions of testimonials that I have and you will be able to start collecting them in whatever ways you find will support your business best.

So, why do businesses need testimonials. Today it is all about social proof and if you don't have social proof, then you are not going to attract the amount of clients that can help you replace your income.

These days people can find just about anything online and if they can't find information about you online, they will be wary about the SERVICES that you provide. Testimonials allow people that you have helped share their gratitude and help you get additional business.

In the old days when a business wanted referrals you had to actually give them like 10 names, addresses and e-mails in order to get the special deal. Most businesses no longer practice this and thank goodness. No one wants to be on the other end of that. What do you think of a friend that gave your information away to a business so that they could get something at a reduced rate? I call these people users. Thank goodness I don't have friends like this today.

Now take a look at the friend who has valued your SERVICES so much that they give you a testimonial. They tell all of their friends about you because of the difference you made in their life. Now instead of ten people who are probably going to dislike the fact that you gave away their information, you are left with people who sincerely want to pass your business information along to others. Testimonials give people the opportunity to tell their friends and the rest of the world the benefits they have received because of working with you. People are all of a sudden touched by this emotionally and want to move forward in doing business with you. They can see that you have benefitted others and they are hoping that you can benefit them as well. Testimonials provide the avenue for your business to grow in a healthy way.

Also, I want you to take a look at testimonials from another viewpoint. Do you enjoy talking about yourself and all of your successes? If you live in the United States, we don't always look highly on people who do this. We call them braggarts. So the amazing things that you could say about yourself and your SERVICES go unsaid because you may not want to be viewed that way, but a testimonial is different. Testimonials allow other people to say what you are able to accomplish in a way that is authentic. It never comes off as a yea right kind of thing because when other people say it, that is their experience. It can't be denied.

Unfortunately for me, I had to learn this the hard way. When I first found out that I could close the reading gap a full year with just 8-12 hours of instruction, I wanted to share that with everyone. But, many people just didn't believe me. Then people started to see what my clients were saying and I never tell people what to say in a testimonial. In fact, I like people to leave their testimonial on LinkedIn, because people will believe the testimonial more.

Here is what one client, Mandy McCumber said.

Joanne Kaminski tutored our 7-year-old daughter in reading this summer. She achieves results that are nothing short of miraculous. In the course of three short months, my daughter's reading improved by 2 1/2 grade levels!

From the first session, we found Joanne to be warm, engaging, and fun. Her enthusiasm for teaching children to read is contagious, and my daughter looked forward to their sessions. Through her blog, Joanne engaged me in the learning process as well. She has some reading tricks that gave my daughter the tools to figure out words by herself, which I believe has set my daughter up for an amazing educational future. Meeting for tutoring sessions through Skype was gentle on the family schedule and very convenient. Her prices are reasonable, and my husband loved that she offered a discount for paying in lump sum.

I only wish we could clone Joanne so she could reach more children. She is gifted. I have no hesitations in recommending her to any parent of a struggling reader.

I only tutored her daughter 1 hour a week and we had these amazing results. Now my social proof has just sky rocketed because of this.

Here is what another client said.

Joanne is an outstanding tutor, with so many creative ways to engage children to improve their reading she's amazing. My son started online reading sessions with Joanne after we discussed his frustrations in reading. He was in 1st grade barely reading at a kindergarten grade level. This was causing social and self esteem issues with him. He worked with Joanne about once a week during two school years. He finished his second grade at an actual second grade reader. Once he started working with Joanne he actually looked forward to the online sessions, because she made reading more fun for him! He clearly became a more confidant reader, and I could not have done it without the extra help from Joanne. I would recommend Joanne as a tutor to anyone who asked.

Then there is more. Here is what another client said.

Joanne has succeeded with my son where other educators have not. Her individual focus allows insight into the best learning style for my child and she has the ability to create a structure that keeps him motivated. His reading has improved tremendously as a direct result of her efforts. We are truly blessed and thankful to have Joanne and I wholeheartedly recommend her to any parent who has a son or daughter struggling with reading.

An adult client shared her story with me and I simply asked her if she would be willing to put a recommendation on LinkedIn. She said that she would love to and here it is.

Joanne was willing to step outside of her normal world and take on an Adult student (myself). She works with me on the thing I need to work on and keeps us on track to use time well. I love that it is so easy to do by Skype! Joanne can be more than just a tutor, it's hard to explain as an adult with Dyslexia she has become a sort of life coach and healer. She is very observant and will find the things that you need to help you how you want and need to be helped.

Only good things have come from the time that Joanne has worked with me in this Skype Tutoring! Just as a person I can't say enough good things about her. Then add that she is the best at what she does for anyone with reading trouble! She will find a way to help! Working with Joanne continues to empower me, that I know I can do these things that I struggled with for so long.
Thank you Joanne for being you!
I Recommend Joanne to anyone looking for a reading tutor for any reason!!!!!
A loyal customer, Renee Love

I am so proud of the amount of progress that Renee has made. She started off thinking that she was reading at a fifth grade level. Now she confidently reads high school and college level material. Before working with me she couldn't get a job and was selling Tupperware to make an income. She is an amazing illustrator, so now she works with me and does all of my graphic design work.

What I love about using LinkedIn as a place for people to put their testimonials is that if they are on LinkedIn, a picture of them comes up. These are real people sharing their experience with me as an online reading tutor.

Here is the thing. The people that you help, don't know how they can help you other than pay their bill. So, all you have to do is ask them what you would like them to do and they will be happy to do it for you. When people give me feedback in an e-mail sharing how I have been helpful to their child, I thank them ask if they would be willing to share a recommendation on LinkedIn. Once they say yes, I send them a request. Usually within a week, the people happily write the recommendation.

You will find these days that testimonials not only happen in the written form, but also in video. Not everyone is willing to capture a testimonial with you on video, but some will be willing to.

The thing with capturing it on video is that it is even more powerful in my mind than a written testimonial. Above, Renee shared her story about Skype tutoring in words. Go to this link to see her video testimonial

http://www.youtube.com/watch?v=E0V0BKIwars.

The video is about 10 minutes long, which people might not want to invest there time into, but if they do, they will be moved with more emotion than they would be from the written testimonial.

Some of you may be thinking, but I have never taught online before, so I don't have anyone that can give me a testimonial. That doesn't mean that you can't sell your SERVICES without one. In fact, when I got started I had the President of the School that I taught in give a recommendation. Here is what she had to say.

I have never met anyone as enthusiastic about teaching children to read as Joanne! Her ability to engage children in ways that facilitate a love of reading is impressive. Joanne is organized and hard-working with a positive attitude. She is also innovative and always thinking of new and different ways to do the work that she loves. Joanne is a literacy expert!

If people that you have worked with in the past are willing to leave a recommendation for you, and you use these testimonials on your website, then people will be more apt to hire you, than if you didn't. People don't want to invest their hard earned dollar on someone that doesn't have anyone vouching for them and what they are able to do.

Write down the names of the people that you could ask for a testimonial that supports what you want to do as an online tutor. Next, contact them and see if they would be willing to help you out.

1. _____
2. _____
3. _____
4. _____
5. _____

12 How to get found without paying a dime

The advice that I am going to give you in this section and the common advice from unsuccessful people running their business is not going to be the same on this topic of how to get found without paying a dime. Now, I tried the unsuccessful process first and will share with you what that is, and then I will share with you what I have done and how it is so much more effective.

Unsuccessful people will tell you to go onto every single tutoring SERVICE website like WizIQ and TutorVista so that you put yourself in front of people looking for tutoring SERVICES. While this strategy may work for some, it doesn't work for most of us. See, they charge you to get on the top pages so that you stand out from the massive amounts of other people out there trying to do what you are doing. It may work if you pay the monthly fee or are willing to give up a portion of your income per student. I didn't feel comfortable with this, so I didn't pay and I didn't get found.

Personally I like to try things before I invest money in them. If what they suggest doesn't work out on the free version, then I am not willing to pay them for the paid version. This is similar to a car dealership, right? If I go to a car dealership I can expect them to let me drive the car off of the lot to see if it works the way I would like it to. If I put the key into the ignition and all of a sudden it didn't start, then I would probably run away from the car dealership as fast as I could.

I personally value my time and I am sure that you do to. Now, you may have had success with these sites, but I am willing to bet that you have probably only had a few students or leads and not enough to make it a full time income. The suggestions that I am going to give away to you in this chapter have been the result of studying successful Marketers, reading tons of books, and seeing how I could do this easily without handing over big chunks of my income.

One of the most common misperceptions out there today is that people will find you by accident in the online world. In fact, I have had several people tell me that they expect people to find them by accident online. In the online world nothing is found by accident. In fact, if you type "online tutoring" in Google there are 29,200,000 results. Do you think amongst all of that garbage that people are going to find you?

On YouTube alone 8 years of content are uploaded each day. So, if you think that people are going to find your one little website by accident, you are going to have to think again. I once paid a company $1,000 to do my SEO for me. They promised to get me on the first page results in Google. Honestly, it doesn't have to cost you that much to do it yourself. The good news is, I can help you to be strategic, get found, and not pay $1,000 to do it. By the end of this chapter you will have keywords and know what to do with those keywords to get found without having to spend any additional money and have people find you because you are the solution to their problem.

How to Figure out your Keywords

First ask everyone you know the following question and write down their answers below.

If you had a child that was struggling with (add what you want to teach online), what would you type into Google?

_____

_____

_____

_____

_____

_____

_____

_____

_____

_____

_____

_____

The answers that people honestly give you regarding this will lead you to some great keywords. Now I want you to brainstorm all of the words that you think would be words people would type in.

_____

_____

_____

_____

_____

_____

_____

_____

_____

_____

_____

I want you to add to your list your name and the name of your company. People will type in your name when they are researching you online, so you want there to be stuff for them to find. If you are going to be tutoring online it only makes sense that people will be able to find content that you put out there whether it be from your blog, articles that you write, guest posts you write for other blogs and so on and so forth.

Think about if there are specific times of year that people tend to need your SERVICES more. For me, people are always looking for reading help in the summer and at back to school season. So I can use these key words in my Marketing to attract people typing these kinds of things in. I met a lady who focuses on math and she tends to have clients that are struggling when it comes time to study for tests or before the SAT or ACT. So, it would be prevalent for her to add these keywords in her list.

Think of other possible ways that people may refer to the type of tutoring you are providing. For example, some countries don't call it math tutoring, but rather maths tutoring. If you are looking to tutor kids in math in the U.K. this is going to be important. I love the time difference between the U.K and the U.S because when it is daytime for me, it is evening for them. So, I am able to work with these clients when my kids are in school.

Next I want you to think about if you are going to provide any in-home tutoring. I have four clients that come to my home for tutoring, so I am able to use the words Wisconsin, Sussex, and Milwaukee in my keywords.

Last we are going to grow this keyword list even bigger. Go to ubersuggest.org. Start typing all of your keywords that you have found so far into the search bar. This program is going to begin giving you suggestions of other keywords to think about. Write down the ones that grab your attention for whatever reason. Sometimes it can be a small matter of one word that will make all of the difference in finding a great keyword.

_____

_____

_____

_____

_____

_____

_____

_____

_____

_____

_____

By this point you should have a ton of potential keywords. In the beginning it is better to have too many than not enough because now we are going to dwindle them down. I want you to take all of the keywords that you think are great keywords and enter them on the Table 1 on the next page under all keywords. Leave the top keywords on this page blank for now.

Table 3

Keyword(s)	Google Adwords	Exact Search in Google	Competition
Top Keywords			

All Keywords

Now go to the Google adword keyword tool[27]. This is a free tool, so if you don't have a Google account at this point, then you will need to create one.

In Figure 3 take a look at the section that says "Match types." On your page click on the box that says exact and make sure the other areas are left unchecked. You want to do research on your keywords to find out what would happen if someone put that keyword into Google exactly.

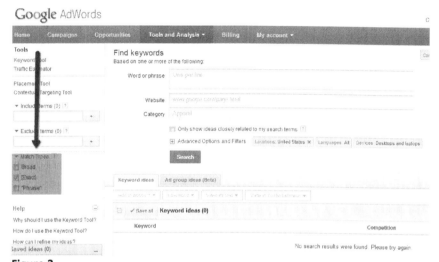

Figure 3

Now you are going to type in your first keyword on your list in the box that says word or phrase, as seen in Figure 4.

---

[27] https://adwords.Google.com/

Figure 4

If you take a look at the red box you will notice that the competition is high and that each month there are about 880 people typing that phrase into the Google toolbar to find something out about online math tutoring. That seems pretty good, right? Now let's see what the actual results look like on Google.

You will notice that there is a triangle that points down next to the keyword and it's results in Figure 5.

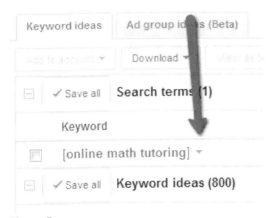

Figure 5

Click on it and you will see some different choices in Figure 6.

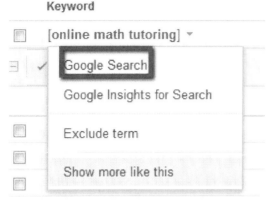

Figure 6

Now click on Google Search and you will be brought to the real search results page in Figure 7.

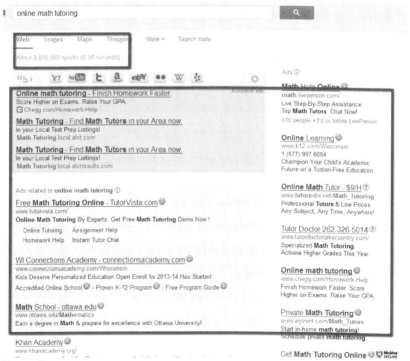

Figure 7

The page in Figure 7 shows that there are 8,800,000 results that pertain to online math tutoring. Wow, those are some pretty scary numbers. Can you really stand out amongst that? No. But, you want to know what the exact results are, so if you go to the search bar and add quotation marks before online and after tutoring, this will give you different results and the ones that will benefit you the most.

"online math tutoring"

Web   Images   Maps   Shopping   More ▾   Search tools

About 6,600,000 results (0.44 seconds)

Figure 8

Figure 8 show that there are 6,600,000 people typing in this keyword exactly. The magic numbers that you are looking for are up to 600,000. You will want to track your results to see what the best keywords are going to be for you like in Table 1.

Table 4

Keyword(s)	Google Adwords	Exact Search in Google	Competition
Top Keywords			

	All Keywords		
online math tutoring	880	6,600,000	high

So, I have the keyword on Table 1 listed as online math tutoring. In the Google Adwords column I put 880. The exact search in Google was 6,600,000. The competition was high. Now, I want the competition to be high, but not with that number. That number is scary.

Let's try the next keyword and see what happens. The next one is "best online math tutoring". The results with just one word, have significantly changed.

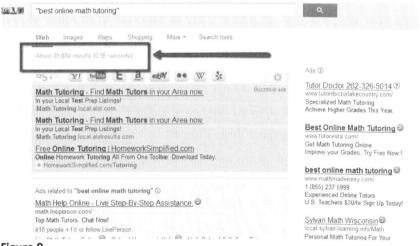

Figure 9

As you can see in Figure 9 there are 98,000 search results. Remember that I want that number to be anywhere up to 600,000. This search result meets that requirement. When you look in Google Adwords, 12 people a month actually type this exact keyword into Google. Not bad.

Another thing to take into consideration when you are choosing keywords is how many people are paying top dollar for ad space. As you can see there are a ton of people paying for this keyword. This one is definitely a great one. This is why you continue to go through this process with all of your keywords. The keywords that come closest to 100,000 and 600,000 that people are paying ad space for, are ones that are going to go into your top keyword space.

So let's take a look at one more example in Figure 10 that is even better than the last one. The keyword I typed in was "online math tutors". This keyword has 260 people typing this keyword in each month. When you visit the results page, this is what it looks like.

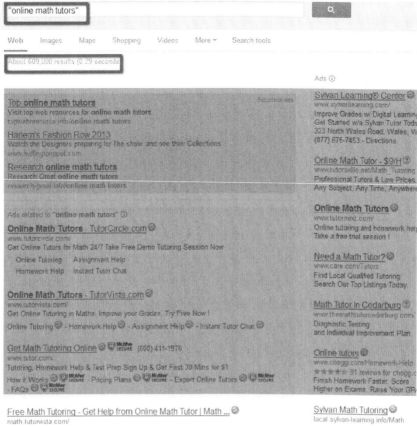

Figure 10

There are 609,000 results. That is a good number. you also want you to take a look at the red area. These are all the people that are paying for this keyword. You want this keyword if you are an online math tutor. Put this in the top keyword section.

This is how simple it is to get found strategically on accident. You find out what search terms people are using to find you as their solution and then you simply do the research to see what are the best ones with the best performance records.

I have taken my keywords and put a copy of them on my wall so that I have easy reference to them. Whenever I am asked to enter keywords into my website, blog page, or blog posts I use these keywords. When I think of articles and books to write, I use these keywords to get those people strategically and accidentally into my sales funnel.

Step 4
SERVICES

13 Free Assessment and Free Report

One of my secret strategies that has worked for me when it comes to providing top notch SERVICES is that I give each of my clients a free assessment. Some of you might be thinking, "Why in the world would you give away a $200 SERVICE for free?" Well, the answer is simple, it doesn't really cost me anything except for a little bit of time and it helps to build rapport.

Other tutoring companies will do an assessment, come up with a plan with the family, and then the family decides they don't have that kind of money to invest in these SERVICES. However, when I give away the assessment and tell them they can try their first session for free, they feel that this is something that they can try.

Think about it like this. You go to a car dealership and they say if you would like to try out this car, then you are going to have to pay $200 plus the gas. What would your response to this person be?

If you are like me, then your response is no thank you. So, you go to another dealership and you say, "Look I just want to test drive this car and see if it works." The salesman says, "Sure, here are the keys. I hope you like it." There is no hassle, taking a test drive was easy, you like the car, you decide to put down the money and pay for it.

We live in a society today that likes to test things before we buy them. Why? Because there is a lot of junk out there and we don't want to get stuck with junk, things that don't work, or SERVICES that don't work.

From the very moment that your potential clients make contact with you, you want to deliver the most personable experience that you can. You are being watched and people will buy SERVICES from people they feel like they know, like, and trust. So be that person that people can know, like, and trust.

By giving away the assessment, people begin to think of you as a caring person. We like caring people and we want to do business with caring people.

Here is a great business philosophy that I put into practice for the assessment that I give. Business philosophy #1 = Under promise and Over deliver.

This means that when you give the assessment report about the child you want to give them so much information that if they decided to go with someone else, they could give your assessment to them and they would be able to replicate what you do. Why? Because caring about that many details on your assessment will not overwhelm a parent in doing nothing, it will drive them to do business with you. They won't want to do business with anyone else. They will have the trust in you that you will be able to fill an educational need for their child.

So here is the secret formula that I use for all of my assessment reports.
>   Introduction
>   Assessment results with graphs and text explaining the results
>   Overall Observations
>   Instructional plan

This formula can be used with any type of tutoring that you provide.

Introduction

The introduction is a place where you can relay the information that you have received from the parent through phone conversations, e-mail, and the registration form. Right off the bat start with the child and what has been revealed to you as the problem. From the beginning of the report you are acknowledging the problems as the parent understands them. This shows that I have been paying attention to their specific child's needs, and helps explain why I have given the child the specific assessments that I have given.

Here is an example of an introduction for a recent client.

Child A is a 5^(th) grade student in Canada going into 6^(th) grade in the fall. He has been struggling with reading since Kindergarten and diagnosed with ADHD in second grade. He has also been diagnosed with a broad based learning disability. His school has been utilizing the Barton Reading and Spelling program and his parents have been helping Child A with this at home. According to Parent A, Child A's dad, he is on level 3.

Child A has had many different tutors that have tried to help him with his reading. Unfortunately, they have been unable to really help Child A succeed. He has made minimal progress and as a direct result does not enjoy reading or having to read. He does not feel comfortable with reading out loud in class and only is asked to do so when he has a book report to do.

Child A has had an online reading tutor previously that was injured an unable to work in the school. She was a classroom teacher for 25 years and had tons of previous experiences that she lists on her website. After working with Child A for 4 days a week for a month the family was unable to see any drastic improvement and discontinued her SERVICES.

Child A has suffered with his reading for a long time and still has hopes and dreams to become a pilot. His dad does not see college being in Child A's future due to his difficulties with learning. However, both mom and dad want to see Child A succeed no matter what his future holds and believe that knowing how to read at a certain level is a priority.

Parent A has been told that Child A is reading at a 2nd grade level. He has noticed that Child A guesses a lot when he reads and that his decoding ability is very weak. Below are the observations about Child A and his current reading level.

From this introduction can you tell that I have been paying attention to the needs of the child and the family. I address everything piece of information that is relevant to this child and his instruction.

Results

Now, the easy part is going through the assessment and providing the results. I will give you an example of one of my assessments, but if you don't tutor in reading, think about what this part could look like for you.

Phonological Awareness

Child A was able to easily find rhyming words, identify rhyming words, and produce rhyming words.

Child A was also able to put two sound and three sounds together to figure out a word, but struggled when it came to 4 sounds and 5 sounds. This is a task that most 2nd graders are able to complete without any problems. Students who struggle with this task that are in the 5th grade usually have dyslexia.

Sight Words

Child A has a huge gap in his ability to read sight words. The program that he is receiving instruction from currently focuses highly on phonics and does not include strategies for figuring out sight words. This helps explain why he is at the Kindergarten instructional level for sight words.

Child A's other learning disabilities and information from his dad suggest that Child A may have some long term memory issues that make it difficult for him to remember words that he has learned from one session to the next. Joanne is going to keep a close eye on this to see how it may affect the sessions that she has designed for him.

	Independent	Instructional	Frustration
Pre-Primer		X	
Primer		X	
1st grade		X	
2nd grade			X

Sight Word Analysis

One thing that the assessor noticed about Child A's reading is that he was able to read the closed pattern words pretty well. He seemed to struggle with sight words, words that do not seem to fit any of the vowel patterns and multisyllabic words.

Child A tends to use the beginning and ends of the words to figure them out. About 96% of the time he is using the beginning and 58% of the time he is using the end. The area that Child A struggles with the most is the middle. This is usually where the vowel is located or the vowel patterns determined.

This data is in correlation with the level that Child A is at with the Barton method. He has progressed through level 1 phonemic awareness and level 2 consonants and short vowels. He is currently on level 3 where the focus is closed patterns and units. He will do well with the method of teaching that Joanne uses because she continues to work with these patterns, but also work with sight words in a way that will help him progress with his reading.

Correct Word	Error	Beginning	Middle	End
what	wit	x		x
animal	amil	x		x
were	where	x		x
want	went	x		x
who	how			
write	worked	x		
place	please	x		x
bear	beer	x		x
find	fund	x		x
sound	sond	x		x
thought	thogunt	x		x
knew	know	x		x
afraid	after	x		
moving	mon	x		
tired	teered	x	x	x
pieces	passes	x		x
picked	pitchered	x		x
though	thug	x		
clue	culg	x		
breathes	birth	x		

insects	insent	x		
weather	wither	x		x
noticed	nots	x		
money	morning	x		
		96%	4%	58%

Words in Context

Child A read Kindergarten words at an Independent level. Words in context at the first grade level however were frustrational for him.

	Independent	Instructional	Frustration
Pre-primer	x		
Primer	x		
1ˢᵗ grade			x

Words in Context Error Analysis

While reading words in text Child A relied significantly on the beginning of the word. About 83% of the time he had the correct beginning sound. When reading in context vs. isolation he relied less on the end of the word. He also identified that he did not know the word and didn't have a strategy for the word in some cases.

When the whole page was text Child A seemed to be easily overwhelmed. He was quickly relieved when the assessor told him that she would not have him read another passage after the 1ˢᵗ grade passage.

Correct Word	Error	Beginning	Middle	End
me	my	x		
spring	summer	x		
then	they	x		
man	mad	x		
kitchen	chen		x	x
heard	Had/hadn't/hold	x		
decided	Didn't	x		
sell	see	x		
ad	an	x		
paper	pepper	x		x
many	main	x		
wanted	until			
visit	vit	x		
came	can	x		
they	there	x		
heard	had	x		x
afraid	after	x		
try	tear	x		
house	family			

heard	Hadn't	x		
We'll	we	x		
		83%	5%	17%

Comprehension 6-16-12

Child A's comprehension seemed to be heavily linked to how well he read the passage. If he read most of the words correctly, then he was able to answer the questions without a problem. The more errors he had the less he was able to understand what he was reading.

	Independent	Instructional	Frustration
Pre-Primer	x		
Primer	x		
1st			x

So that is the actual assessment from one of my students. I know everything that this child is able to do and everything that he needs to know to become a better reader. I have also noticed that the child most likely has dyslexia, which is why he is struggling so much and slowly have started sharing this information through the report.

Overall Observations

The overall observations is a place where you can take the information from the introduction and the information from the assessment to give an overall view of what this child is able to do up to this point. State what the actual reading level is so that the parent doesn't have to guess. Tell parents that if the report is too confusing, all they have to do is look at the introduction, overall observations, and the instructional plan. If the parent needs to know more, then they can certainly look through each of the results, but it is not totally necessary.

Here is an overall observation regarding the same child. This is to give a complete picture for you.

The assessor has noticed that Child A may have dyslexia. An additional diagnoses from a psychologist would only be suggested if it would help to get the SERVICES that Child A would need from school staff to support Child A. Otherwise there would not be a benefit for getting the diagnosis.

Child A is actually reading at an end of the Kindergarten level between his decoding and comprehension skills. It is very probable at one point Child A was reading at a 2nd grade level, but due to the dyslexia has decreased in his ability.

Child A seemed to enjoy working on reading on the computer. Even though he was asked to do some activities that were difficult he cooperated every step of the way.

Child A struggles with being able to read sight words because he is not currently engaged in a reading program that focuses on them. He also struggles with reading words that do not fall into the closed pattern. Child A will benefit from a reading program that focuses on both sight words and phonics patterns along with reading lots of text.

Child A has been struggling with reading for a long time and his self-esteem has been affected as well. With Child A going to the 6th grade in the fall he will benefit from reading a lot of non-fiction text. This way he will not be reading books that seem to be too babyish for his intellect.

Some parents even use this as a tool with the school system to get additional help for their child. This is fantastic. Once the classroom teacher sees the amount of information that the parent now has regarding their child, they become more empowered to be an advocate for their child.

Instructional Plan

On the assessment I don't go into huge details about what instruction I will be providing, but just the activities that will occur. Here is Child A's instructional plan.

Sight Words

Vowel Pattern Chart

Reading Practice and Comprehension with RAZ kids

That is it. It simply states the tools that the instructor will use. You don't have to go into detail on that part. The most important part is already in the parent's hand. The report identifies the problem, and now that the assessor has clearly defined that problem and has a plan to fix it. At this point the assessor becomes the solution for the parent.

Conclusion

This assessment is a peek into the amazing quality SERVICES that you will be providing their child. Clearly, people that are able to come off in this kind of professional manner are going to be successful in their tutoring business and stand out against anyone else out there. Begin thinking how you can construct an assessment for the clients that you will be helping. This formula can be used for any subject.

14 Connecting with your students

Tutoring students online is only part of what you do to provide quality SERVICES. "Whatever you do, make sure you do it well," right? There is another component to your tutoring SERVICES that will make you stand out from the crowd, get you noticed, and get you more referrals.

What is that you may be thinking? Well, it is authentically connecting with your students. Your students could be watching t.v., playing with their friends, or doing anything else but hanging out with you on the computer. If you are not connecting with them, then they are not going to enjoy coming to their sessions and they are going to fight with their parents to begin their tutoring. When this kind of resistance exists, parents stop paying for the SERVICE.

I have found that I just don't always connect well with all kids, but I make an effort every single day. In this chapter you are going to learn about the things that you can do to connect and engage with the students and the students parents to be satisfied with the SERVICES that you are providing them.

Tip #1 – If there is another kid or animal in the background, make note of it.

Personalize the time that you have with each of your students. Most likely you will be able to hear sounds in the background that will open the door for that child to connect with you. If you hear that the child has siblings in the background ask them how old they are and what their names are. That way when they come up to the computer you can greet them by their name instead of referring to them as sister or brother. You can easily write this information down on the cover of the child's folder. That way, anytime you hear the brother in the background you can say something like, "Oh sounds like Joey is having a lot of fun today." That usually gets the child laughing or a little smile. You can usually figure out the relationship the sibling has because of the look on his/her face. Then you connect with that.

I don't know of any kids that don't love their pets. If you hear that there is a dog in the background, then you can ask what kind of dog the child has. Ask the child the name of the pet and if you can't determine if it is a boy or a girl, then ask. That way when you hear Marley in the background you say something like, "Did you get to play with Marley today?"

Tip #2 – Tell your student that he or she is not allowed to smile.

Seriously, say this with the most sincere (not mean) tone that you can. Your student will begin laughing and smiling instantly. Then you follow it all up with, "Hey, I told you no smiling." This get's them in a good mood in no time.

If the parents can see that their child is smiling and having fun, even if the child didn't want to tutor, they feel like they are leaving their child in capable hands. At the end of the day, parents want their kids to have fun and if you can engage their child and make it fun for them, then they view the SERVICES that you are providing as a worthwhile investment.

Tip #3 – Smile

It is amazing how one little smile from you can spark a smile from the child. I love greeting the child with a smile. This is one of the reasons I tell them they can't smile if they are not smiling when we get onto the session together. This automatically changes the

MINDSET for the child, where they may have had a bad day before they get on the computer with you, now they are ready to learn.

I often have kids surprised that their time is up already after a half hour. Most of the time it is because I try to make it as fun as I can.

Tip #4 – Give your student choices

Anytime that you can give a child choices will result in a child that is more engaged than if you make all of the choices. My students that need to work on sight words are not allowed to make choices about that activity, but I have different background slides they can choose and they love choosing what their background is going to be. This little personalization makes the entire process special.

I always allow my students to choose the book that they want to read as well. I can even ask them why they chose the book and that will give me more information about the child to connect with them about.

Tip #5 – Ask your student about his/her day.

Every time I get on a new session with one of my students I start it off by asking about their day. I usually get the very short response of, "Good." But, I can probe deeper if time allows and say something like, "Tell me about your favorite thing that happened today?" Another good one is, "Did you have a good lunch? What did you have?" I am usually asking these kinds of questions, listening to the response and opening up their materials. It is a great use of time.

Tip #6 – Be genuinely interested in what your student has to tell you.

At certain times your student is going to feel so comfortable with you that he/she will want to share stories with you. Listen with a genuine heart and then get back to the lesson. It usually only takes a minute or two for the child to share his or her excitement with you and this allows you to connect with him/her in a new way.

Kids love sharing information about the sports they are in. They want to share their victories with you because you are an important person to him/her.

These are all great ways to connect with the person on the other end. I do all of this during the lesson and keep my lessons to the time allotted. I am forced to because I have another student scheduled right afterwards usually.

None of these ways of connecting with students actually takes a lot of time, so the time that you invest in them will have big dividends for you. You will come off as personable and likeable. Guess what? People like to do business with people they like, know and trust. So give people a reason to like you by being the most authentic you that you can be. If any of the tips don't feel authentic to you, then try some other ways that do. Trying to be someone that you are not will never make people feel authentically connected to you.

15 Good Communication

People who provide good SERVICES to their clients are good communicators. Not answering phone calls, responding to e-mail messages, or not showing up to a session are all signs of poor communication. If your communication skills are not clear, then you will have sales falling through the cracks of your business. This chapter is broken down into rules. Rules must be followed or their will be consequences and in an online world where people seem to disappear into cyberspace, if you don't follow these rules people will not only discontinue their SERVICES with you, but they also are not about to refer your SERVICES to other people.

Rule #1 Promptly return phone messages

Nothing proves your professionalism than responding to people in a quick manner. In this day and age, people don't expect other people to get back to them within 24 hours. Sometimes it can be days or weeks. However, if you want to stand out from the crowd, then make this a priority and your business will flourish.

Rule #2 Listen to your customer

Your customer is going to reveal a lot about their communication right from the start. People tend to use the type of communication they like to use best. So, if you are receiving e-mails from a client, most likely they prefer that method. If they send you texts, then they prefer that method. Whatever method you receive a message, return the response in that message.

There are so many methods out there today that it is impossible for everyone to keep up with it. But here's the thing. If you expect your client to change their methods to communicate with you because you only use one type of communication, then this is going to lead to poor communication.

What would you expect to happen to a business that has poor communication? It closes down eventually or goes bankrupt, right? Well, the same can happen with your tutoring business.

I have to remember to keep my cell phone with me in my office because some clients will text me that they can't make a session. I have a 24 hour policy, but I also believe in flexibility. Sometimes parents just can't make it home in time and it is not my place to judge. I appreciate that people are trying to communicate with me, so I need to open myself up to listen to their form of communication.

Here are the different forms of communication to get familiar with.
Facebook messages
e-mail
phone
text
Skype instant chat
Google instant chat

Rule #3 Send a welcome packet stating all of the useful information they need to know in the mail

People appreciate being informed. Sending a welcome packet in the mail vs. e-mail is going to do two things. First, it is going to get their attention more amongst all the noise of e-mail and they will be more apt to read it. Second, it is going to show your professionalism. Sometimes e-mails don't have the same professional quality as a packet that is received in the mail.

In the letter you can include
1. Why you are excited to work with them
2. Information about your cancellation policy
3. How often you will assess and give feedback
4. All of the ways that they can communicate with you
5. Payment plan
6. How to cancel SERVICES
7. How to put SERVICES on hold
8. How to reinstate SERVICES
9. Thank them for the opportunity to work with their child

Also in the welcome packet you can put a couple of your business cards. Let people know that if they are happy with your SERVICES and they want to pass these along to others, that you would appreciate it. Referrals are one of the biggest ways that companies stay in business and this is true in the online tutoring world as well. Just think of it, if each of your clients referred you to two people, you could stay in business just off of referrals.

In the packet you can even put a bookmark or something small that will give your new client great tips. Everybody loves free goodies.

Rule #4 – Create a schedule where you assess each of your students every 3 months.

Every 10 weeks the school system provides an overview of how a child is doing. They use the report card. In online tutoring, since the parents are forking over more of their money, they want feedback as well.

However, the parents don't want general feedback like your child is getting much better in understanding what she is reading. They want details that back up how you know they are improving. So, reassess the child every 3 months and then report back to the parents regarding the results. The parents will be grateful that you did..

Rule #5 – Always communicate with your client when you need to cancel a session.

Sometimes things happen in life and you are not able to meet with a student at a certain time. Have blocks of time on your schedule that you are able to do makeup sessions. Here is an example e-mail of not being able to make a session.

Dear Angela,
I am so sorry, but I will not be able to tutor Brendon on Thursday night. My daughter is having her Christmas concert. I do have two other days that might work for you. One is Wednesday night at 7:00 pm and the other is Saturday morning at 10:00 am. Which time would work best for you?

I don't cancel sessions often, but the beauty of having an online business is that it is pretty easy to switch things around. I love it. I don't even really have to put the reason on there as to why I can't make the session. The important thing is that when I am not able to make a session I offer two other times that will work.

In conclusion you want to be as clear in communication with each of your clients as you can, because at the end of the day this is what people who provide good SERVICE do. Remember to communicate with your client in the form of communication they use best and respond quickly. Send a welcome packet to their home that goes through all the details they need to know. Provide ongoing assessments and ongoing feedback to your clients regarding progress. Lastly, contact your clients through their favorite form of communication when you are not able to make a session. These tools are the basis of a good client relationship. Each of your clients deserves the VIP treatment, so give it to them.

16 What your life really could look like

As you have been reading this book you are probably one of two types of people. You are either someone who has already started your own tutoring company at home and are looking for new strategies and ideas, or you are thinking of becoming an online tutor. Either way, congratulations for being a part of this journey.

Online tutoring is a new career path that didn't exist when any of us were children. We are on the cutting edge of technology and it is an exciting place to be. The SEO Keyword chapter is really as technical as our job gets, but it is the most rewarding way to get found online. Those same experiences that you have teaching kids in the classroom and one on one are still the most amazing moments that you will get to experience.

Yesterday I had a dyslexic 3rd grade student begin to make major growth. She has made slow progress, but all of a sudden it has all started to click for her. She is beginning to see patterns and she is reading words that once she wouldn't even attempt. The feeling that I had in my heart was priceless. Seriously, I felt like I was walking on cloud nine. To know that I have really made a difference for this child in ways that other educators couldn't is the most priceless gift that I get to receive on a daily basis and you will get to receive this gift as well.

Most likely you became a teacher for reasons just like this, right? As soon as I had my own children though there was a really big hole in my life. I love my kids more than anything in the world and I was sacrificing that to be of SERVICE to other peoples kids in the classroom. Now I have the best of both worlds. Supermom by day, Supertutor by night and it is all from the comfort of my home.

There really couldn't be a more glorious lifestyle. I can travel the world whenever I want. I don't have to wait for when I have time off of school, which happens to be the busy season for traveling. I can travel to awesome places on the off season and enjoy them without all of the hustle and bustle. I can bring my tutoring company wherever I go. I have the ultimate in flexibility. If I want to take a week off, I just let my clients know. We work it out. There are times like when I took my family to Disney World for Mickey's Spectacular Halloween event and I just wanted to focus on my family. So, I did. I added sessions in during the month to make up for the time that would be lost. It was wonderful as you can see in Figure 11.

Figure 11

I went to the beach in the winter when it is super cold here in Wisconsin and worked a few hours during the day and enjoyed the rest of the time at the beach in San Diego. I got to visit the zoo, Sea World and just soak in the rays. It was awesome.

I get to be home for my kids on the first day every single year, without having to ask someone if I can as in Figure 12.

Figure 12

In Figure 13 you can see that I took my whole family to China and experienced the world in ways I never thought possible.

Figure 13

I took my kids to Disney world in Hong Kong, Figure 14.

Figure 14

We've gotten to experience toilets, Figure 15, that we had no idea even how to use. Those of you that have been to China know what I mean.

Figure 15

I get to be room mom and volunteer in my daughter's schools, Figure 16.

Figure 16

I am a #1 top selling author on Amazon for 31 Days to Become a Better Reader: Increasing your Struggling Reader's Reading Level, Figure 17, all because I have time to write about my passions.

Figure 17

I speak at schools, Figure 18, and motivate kids to read, write and illustrate. The picture below shows me talking to a group of 4th graders about my book Three Little Sisters Learn to Get Along.

Figure 18

I am living a life I couldn't even have dreamed of as a child. Now, I know that my dream life is not what your dream life looks like or what you may want it to look like. We are all different right? So this book isn't going to end with my story. It is going to end with yours. I want you to think about what your dreams are. What do you want to accomplish, how much money do you want to make, where are places that you want to go, who do you want to meet, who do you want to inspire? Do you want to do this with time freedom, financial freedom, and complete flexibility? Then make that part of your story. You can be, do, and have, whatever your heart desires. If you can think it, then you can achieve it. Don't let people who aren't living their dreams sidetrack you from living yours. Teachers have been locked up in classrooms for too long. It is time to break free, do what you love, and get paid what your worth.

17 Now What?

"Happiness is not something that you get once you are successful. Success is a direct result of being happy."

If you are like me, then you don't want this journey that we have had together to end. There is so much more that I want to be able to teach you so that you can be recession and competition proof doing what you love doing.

I mentioned earlier that I have created a community of people that want to support you in your journey. If you decide to join us, then go to www.tutorpreneurs.com/free-videos. Let us stand out as the best tutors all over the world that are the most highly sought out group of educators.

I am sure that people have told you your whole life that teachers don't make a 6-figure income. Well, they don't make it because nobody has ever believed that they can. We are starting a new era here. Without teachers we wouldn't have doctors, lawyers, or presidents. So, let's continue making a difference in the lives of others and in our own lives as well.

Joanne Kaminski

Other books available on Amazon by Joanne Kaminski

31 Days to Become a Better Reader: Increasing your struggling reader's reading level

Phonics the Easy Way

How to Raise Non-Fiction Reading Levels

Three Little Sisters Learn to Get Along

ABOUT THE AUTHOR

Joanne Kaminski is #1 topselling author and recipient of the S.T.A.R. award for her book 31 Days to Become a Better Reader: Increasing your Struggling Reader's Reading Level. She has also written Three Little Sisters Learn to Get Along and How to Raise Non-fiction reading levels. She has been an online reading tutor since 2010 and is able to close the reading gap a full year with just 8-12 hours of instruction.

Joanne is currently teaching kids online, but also teaching teachers how to increase or replace their current income by becoming an online tutor in whatever area of teaching they love the most. Not only are teachers able to learn more than has ever been available to them before about this career choice, but they can also become certified, and receive support every step of the way.

As a mom, wife, friend and daughter Joanne has realized that too much of our time is spent being concerned about the wrong things. Being of SERVICE to her family, friends, students, and other teachers gives her a sense of purpose that others could only dream of.

Made in the USA
Charleston, SC
27 March 2013